MOI

Microsoft®
WINDOWS® 95

Step by Step

Other titles in the Step by Step series:

For Microsoft Windows 95

Microsoft Office 95 Integration Step by Step

Microsoft Access for Windows 95 Step by Step

Microsoft Access/Visual Basic Step by Step

Microsoft Excel for Windows 95 Step by Step

Microsoft Excel/Visual Basic Step by Step

Microsoft PowerPoint for Windows 95 Step by Step

Microsoft Project for Windows 95 Step by Step

Microsoft Visual Basic 4 Step by Step

Microsoft Windows 95 Step by Step

Microsoft Word for Windows 95 Step by Step

Microsoft Works for Windows 95 Step by Step

Upgrading to Microsoft Windows 95 Step by Step

For Microsoft Windows 3.1

Microsoft Access 2 for Windows Step by Step

Microsoft Excel 5 for Windows Step by Step

Microsoft Excel 5 Visual Basic for Applications Step by Step, for Windows

Microsoft Visual FoxPro 3 for Windows Step by Step

Microsoft Mail for Windows Step by Step, versions 3.0b and later

Microsoft Office for Windows Step by Step, version 4

Microsoft PowerPoint 4 for Windows Step by Step

Microsoft Project 4 for Windows Step by Step

Microsoft Word 6 for Windows Step by Step

Microsoft Works 3 for Windows Step by Step

MORE

Microsoft®

WINDOWS® 95

Step by Step

Microsoft Press

PUBLISHED BY
Microsoft Press
A Division of Microsoft Corporation
One Microsoft Way
Redmond, Washington 98052-6399

Library of Congress Cataloging-in-Publication Data
More Microsoft Windows 95 step by step / Catapult, Inc.
        p.   cm.
    Includes index.
    ISBN 1-55615-888-2
    1. Microsoft Windows (Computer file)   I. Catapult, Inc.
QA76.76.W56M658   1996
005.4'3--dc20   95-38802
                                                                          CIP

Printed and bound in the United States of America.

1 2 3 4 5 6 7 8 9   QMQM   9 8 7 6

Distributed to the book trade in Canada by Macmillan of Canada, a division of Canada
Publishing Corporation.

A CIP catalogue record for this book is available from the British Library.

Microsoft Press books are available through booksellers and distributors worldwide. For further
information about international editions, contact your local Microsoft Corporation office. Or
contact Microsoft Press International directly at fax (206) 936-7329.

For Catapult, Inc.
Managing Editor: Donald Elman
Writer: Steve Matlock
Project Editor: Ann T. Rosenthal
Production/Layout Editor: Jeanne K. Hunt
Technical Editor: Brett R. Davidson
Indexer: Julie Kawabata

For Microsoft Press
Acquisitions Editor: Casey D. Doyle
Project Editor: Laura Sackerman

Catapult, Inc. & Microsoft Press

More Microsoft Windows 95 Step by Step has been created by the professional trainers and writers at Catapult, Inc., to the exacting standards you've come to expect from Microsoft Press. Together, we are pleased to present this self-paced training guide, which you can use individually or as part of a class.

Catapult, Inc. is a software training company with years of experience in PC and Macintosh instruction. Catapult's exclusive Performance-Based Training system is available in Catapult training centers across North America and at customer sites. Based on the principles of adult learning, Performance-Based Training ensures that students leave the classroom with confidence and the ability to apply skills to real-world scenarios. *More Microsoft Windows 95 Step by Step* incorporates Catapult's training expertise to ensure that you'll receive the maximum return on your training time. You'll focus on the skills that increase productivity the most while working at your own pace and convenience.

Microsoft Press is the independent—and independent-minded—book publishing division of Microsoft Corporation. The leading publisher of information on Microsoft software, Microsoft Press is dedicated to providing the highest quality end-user training, reference, and technical books that make using Microsoft software easier, more enjoyable, and more productive.

Contents at a Glance

Table of Contents

Table of Contents

Table of Contents

QuickLook Guide

Installing additional Windows 95 components, see Lesson 1, page 3

Finding and fixing common disk problems, see Lesson 3, page 46

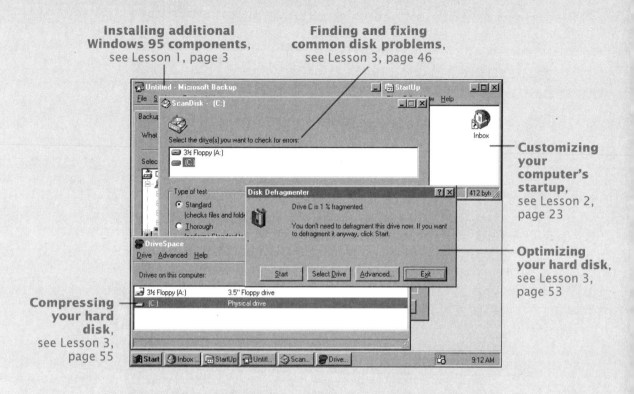

Customizing your computer's startup, see Lesson 2, page 23

Optimizing your hard disk, see Lesson 3, page 53

Compressing your hard disk, see Lesson 3, page 55

Working with networks and servers, see Lesson 4, page 68

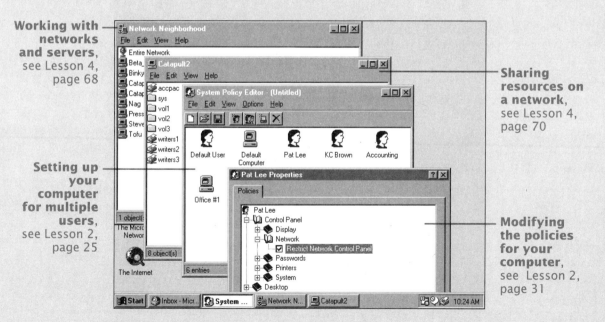

Sharing resources on a network, see Lesson 4, page 70

Setting up your computer for multiple users, see Lesson 2, page 25

Modifying the policies for your computer, see Lesson 2, page 31

Reading and posting messages to bulletin boards, see Lesson 5, page 105

Connecting to The Microsoft Network, see Lesson 5, page 100

Sending and receiving e-mail, see Lesson 6, page 118

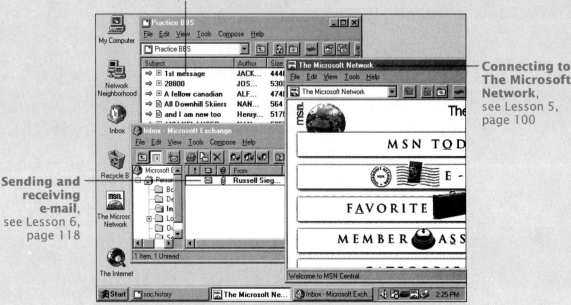

Sending and receiving faxes, see Lesson 7, page 137

Using folders to organize your mail, see Lesson 6, page 122

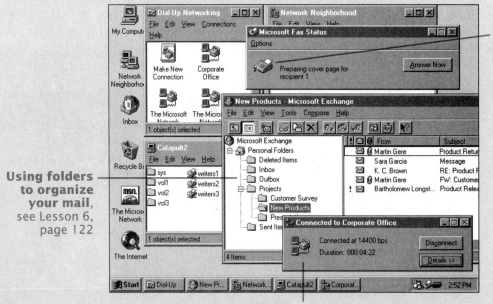

Connecting to a remote computer using Dial-Up Networking, see Lesson 7, page 131

Using Sound Recorder to create and play sound files, see Lesson 8, page 162

Using the Media Player, see Lesson 8, page 158

Playing audio CDs on your CD-ROM drive, see Lesson 9, page 172

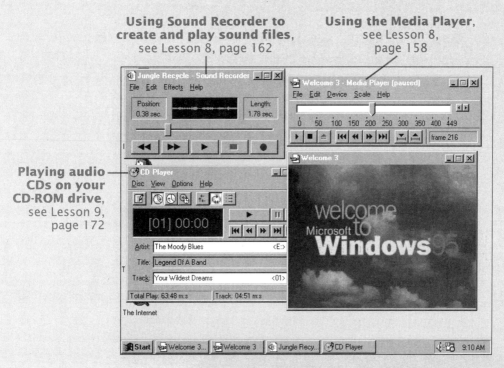

Modifying the appearance of your Desktop using Desktop Themes, see Lesson 10, page 190

Editing the play list for an audio CD, see Lesson 9, page 174

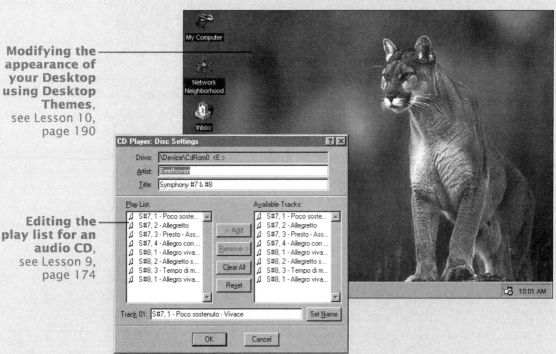

*Quick*Look Guide

Browse through the Internet using The Microsoft Network, see Lesson 11, page 219

Relaxing with 3-D Pinball, see Lesson 11, page 223

Using DriveSpace 3 to compress your disk, see Lesson 10, page 199

Working with the System Agent to schedule tasks, see Lesson 10, page 197

Browsing through Internet newsgroups, see Lesson 11, page 213

Creating Internet shortcuts, see Lesson 11, page 226

Posting messages to Internet newsgroups, see Lesson 11, page 218

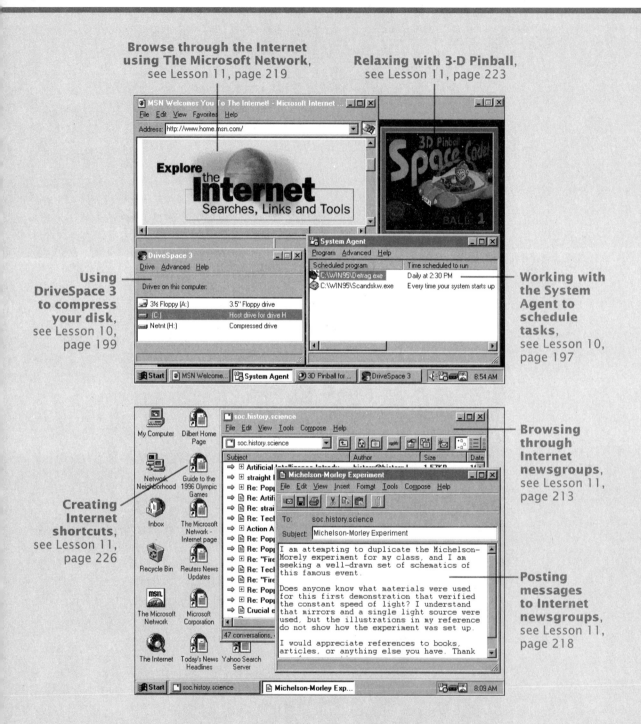

About This Book

In "About This Book" you will:

- Find your best starting point in this book based on your level of experience.
- Learn what the conventions used in this book mean.
- Learn where to get additional information about Windows 95.

More Microsoft Windows 95 Step by Step is designed for users of Windows 95 who want to quickly learn and apply more of the advanced features of Windows 95 to their work. With this book, you'll learn how to set up, customize, and manage your system resources; communicate through local and remote networks; and use multimedia and Microsoft Plus! all at your own pace and at your own convenience. You can also use this book in a classroom setting.

You get hands-on practice by using the practice files on the disk located in the back of this book. Each lesson explains when and how to use the appropriate practice files. Instructions for copying the practice files to your computer hard disk are in "Getting Ready," the next chapter in this book.

Finding the Best Starting Point for You

This book is divided into four major parts, each containing two or more related lessons. Each lesson takes approximately 20 to 45 minutes. At the end of each part is a Review & Practice section that gives you the opportunity to practice the skills you learned in that part. Each Review & Practice section allows you to test your knowledge and prepare for your own work.

Everyone should first follow the instructions for installing the practice files in "Getting Ready," the next chapter in this book. You can work through the parts of the book in any order, depending on your interests, but it is recommended that you work consecutively through the lessons in each part. If a specific, installable component is required for a lesson, installation instructions will be given at the beginning of the lesson. Before you do Part 2 or Part 4, you should work through Part 1, "Managing Your Files and Drives" for administrative and configuration functions that you'll need to be familiar with.

Using This Book As a Classroom Aid

If you're an instructor, you can use *More Microsoft Windows 95 Step by Step* for teaching Windows 95 users about the advanced features of Windows 95. You might want to select certain lessons that meet your students' particular needs and incorporate your own demonstrations into the lessons.

If you plan to teach the entire contents of this book, you should set aside two days of classroom time to allow for discussion, questions, and any customized practice you might create.

Conventions Used in This Book

Before you start any of the lessons, it's important that you understand the terms and notational conventions used in this book.

Procedural Conventions

- Hands-on exercises that you are to follow are given in numbered lists of steps (1, 2, and so on). An arrowhead bullet (▶) indicates an exercise that has only one step.

- Characters or commands that you type appear in **bold** characters.

Print

- You can carry out many commands by clicking the buttons at the top of a program window. If a procedure in this book instructs you to click a button, a picture of the button appears in the left margin, as the Print button does here.

Mouse Conventions

- If you have a multiple-button mouse, it is assumed that you have configured the left mouse button as the primary mouse button. Any procedure that requires you to click the secondary button will refer to it as the right mouse button.

- *Click* means to point to an object and then press and release the mouse button. For example, "Click the Cut button on the Standard toolbar." *Use the right mouse button to click* means to point to an object and then press and release the right mouse button.

- *Drag* means to point to an object and then press and hold down the mouse button while you move the mouse. For example, "Drag the window edge downward to enlarge the window."

■ *Double-click* means to rapidly press and release the mouse button twice. For example, "Double-click the My Computer icon to open the My Computer window."

Keyboard Conventions

■ Names of keyboard keys that you are instructed to press are in small capital letters, for example, TAB and SHIFT.

■ A plus sign (+) between two key names means that you must press those keys at the same time. For example, "Press ALT+TAB" means that you hold down the ALT key while you press TAB.

■ Procedures generally emphasize use of the mouse, rather than the keyboard. However, you can choose menu commands with the keyboard by pressing the ALT key to activate the menu bar and then sequentially pressing the keys that correspond to the highlighted or underlined letter of the menu name and then the command name. For some commands, you can also press a key combination listed in the menu.

Notes

■ Notes or Tips that appear either in the text or the left margin provide additional information or alternative methods for a procedure.

■ Notes labeled "Important" alert you to essential information that you should check before continuing with the lesson.

■ Notes labeled "Warning" alert you to possible data loss and tell you how to proceed safely.

Other Features of This Book

■ The "One Step Further" exercise at the end of each lesson introduces new options or techniques that build on the commands and skills you used in the lesson.

■ Each lesson concludes with a Lesson Summary that lists the skills you have learned in the lesson and briefly reviews how to accomplish particular tasks. You can use the summary as a quick reference guide after completing the lesson.

■ The "Review & Practice" activity at the end of each part provides an opportunity to use the major skills presented in the lessons for that part. These activities present problems that reinforce what you have learned and demonstrate new ways you can use Windows 95.

■ The Glossary toward the end of the book provides a useful reference for terms and concepts covered in the book.

References to Windows 95 Online Help

References to Microsoft Windows 95 online Help at the end of each lesson direct you to specific Help topics for additional information. The Help system in Windows 95 provides a complete online reference to Windows 95. You'll learn more about the Help system in Getting Ready, the next chapter in this book.

Getting Ready

In "Getting Ready" you will learn:

- How to copy the practice files to your computer hard disk.
- How to find the information you need by using the Windows 95 Help system.

This chapter prepares you for your first steps into using this book and finding information when you need it. You will install the practice files that come with this book, and you'll get an introduction to the Windows 95 Help system, which you can use while you work to learn more about the features and functions in Windows 95.

IMPORTANT   This book is designed for use with the Windows 95 operating system with a Custom setup and all components installed. If a specific, installable component is required for a lesson, installation instructions will be given at the beginning of the lesson.

Installing the Step by Step Practice Files

The disk attached to the inside back cover of this book contains practice files that you'll use as you work through this book. You'll use the practice files in many of the lessons to perform the exercises. For example, the lesson that teaches you how to play a waveform audio file instructs you to find and open a waveform practice file. Because the practice files simulate tasks you'll encounter in a typical business setting, you can easily transfer what you learn from this book to your own work.

Copy the practice files to your hard disk

You must have Microsoft Windows 95 installed on your computer to use the practice files. Follow these steps to copy the practice files to your computer hard disk so that you can use them with the lessons.

If you do not know your user name or password, contact your system administrator for further help.

1   If your computer isn't already on, turn it on now. If you see a dialog box asking for your user name and password, type them in the appropriate boxes and then click OK. If you see the Welcome dialog box, click the Close button.

My Computer icon

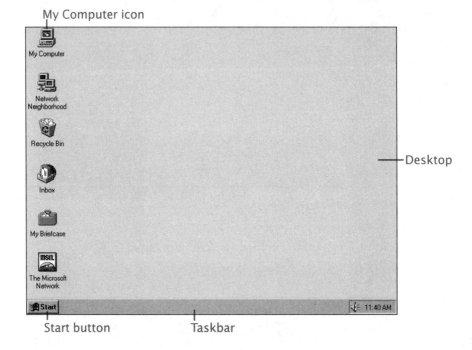

Desktop

Start button   Taskbar

2   Remove the disk from the package on the inside back cover of this book.

3   Put the disk in drive A or drive B of your computer.

4   On the taskbar at the bottom of your screen, click the Start button.

5   On the Start menu, click Run.

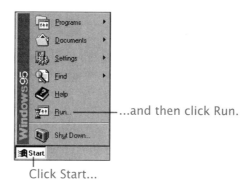

...and then click Run.

Click Start...

6 In the Run dialog box, type **a:setup** (or **b:setup** if the disk is in drive B), and then click the OK button. Do not type a space anywhere in the command.

7 Follow the directions on the screen.

The setup program window appears with recommended options preselected for you. For best results in using the practice files with this book, accept the recommendations made by the program.

8 When the files have been copied, remove the disk from your computer and replace it in the envelope on the inside back cover of the book.

You'll need to remember the name of the drive and folder where the practice files are stored so that you can open a file when you are directed in a lesson.

Each lesson in this book explains when and how to use one or more of the practice files for that lesson. When it's time to use a practice file in a lesson, the book will list instructions for how to open the file.

Lesson Background

The lessons in this book are built around a scenario that simulates a real work environment, so you can easily apply the skills you learn to your own work. For this scenario, imagine that you're an employee at Childs Play, Inc., a toy manufacturing company. Most of the time, you work in your home office where you are designing a marketing presentation. As part of your home office tasks, you also need to manage your files and optimize your computer's performance. You'll use online tools, such as e-mail and the Internet, to communicate with your main office. Periodically, you return to the main office where you act as an informal support person to help your co-workers get the most out of Windows 95.

Getting Help with Windows 95

When you're at work and you want to find out more information about how to do a project, you might ask a co-worker or consult a reference book. When you need information about a procedure or how to use a particular feature on your computer, the online Help system is one of the most efficient ways to learn. The online Help system for Windows 95 is available from the Start menu, and you can choose the type of help you want from the Help dialog box.

For instructions on broad categories, you can look at the Help contents. Or, you can search the Help index for information on specific topics. The Help information is short and concise, so you can get the exact information you need quickly. There are also shortcut buttons in many Help topics that you can use to directly switch to the task you want to perform.

Viewing Help Contents

The Help Contents tab is organized like a book's table of contents. As you choose top-level topics, or "chapters," you see a list of more detailed topics from which to choose. Many of these chapters have "Tips and Tricks" subsections to help you work more efficiently.

Find Help on general categories

Suppose you want to learn more about using Calculator, a program that comes with Windows 95. In this exercise, you'll look up information in the online Help system.

1 Click Start. On the Start menu, click Help.

The Help Topics: Windows Help dialog box appears.

2 If necessary, click the Contents tab to make it active.

3 Double-click "Introducing Windows."

A set of subtopics appears.

4 Double-click "Using Windows Accessories."

5 Double-click "For General Use."

6 Double-click "Calculator: for making calculations."

A Help topic window appears.

7 Click the Close button to close the Help window.

Finding Help on Specific Topics

There are two methods for finding specific Help topics: the Index tab and the Find tab. The Index tab is organized like a book's index. Keywords for topics are organized alphabetically. You can either scroll through the list of keywords, or you can type the keyword you want to find. Windows 95 online Help then presents one or more topic choices.

With the Find tab, you can also enter a keyword. The main difference is that you get a list of all Help topics in which that keyword appears, not just the topics that begin with that word.

Find Help on specific topics using the Help index

In this exercise, you'll use the Help index to learn how to change the background pattern of your Desktop.

1 Click Start. On the Start menu, click Help.

The Help dialog box appears.

2 Click the Index tab to make it active.

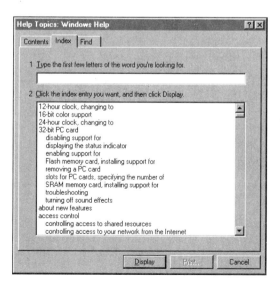

3   In the text box, type **display**

A list of display-related topics appears.

4   Double-click the topic named "background pictures or patterns, changing."

The Topics Found window appears.

5   Double-click the topic named "Changing the background of your Desktop."

6   Read the Help topic.

7   Click the shortcut button in Step 1 of the Help topic.

Shortcut

The Display properties dialog box appears. If you want, you can immediately perform the task you are looking up in Help.

8   Click the Close button on the Display Properties dialog box.

Close

9   Click the Close button on the Windows Help window.

> **NOTE**   You can print any Help topic. Click the Options button in the upper-left corner of any Help topic window, click Print Topic, and then click OK. To continue searching for additional topics, you can click the Help Topics button in any open Help topic window.

Find Help on specific topics using the Find tab

In this exercise, you'll use the Find tab to learn how to change your printer's settings.

1   Click Start. On the Start menu, click Help to display the Help dialog box.

2   Click the Find tab to make it active.

3 If you see a wizard, select the best option for your system, and then click Next. Click Finish to complete and close the wizard.

The wizard creates a search index for your Help files. This might take a few minutes. The next time you use Find, you won't have to wait for Windows 95 to create the list. The Find tab appears.

4 In the text box, type **print**

All topics that have to do with printing are displayed in the list box at the bottom of the tab.

5 In the list box under Step 3, click the "Changing printer settings" topic, and then click Display.

The Help topic appears.

6 Read the Help topic, using the scroll bar as necessary.

7 Click the Close button on the Windows Help window.

Find Help on a dialog box

Almost every dialog box includes a question mark button in the upper-right corner of its window. When you click this button and then click any dialog box control, a Help window appears that explains what the control is and how to use it. In this exercise, you'll get help on specific elements in a dialog box by using pop-up Help.

1 Click Start. On the Start menu, click Run.

The Run dialog box appears.

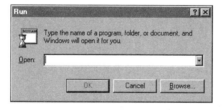

2 Click the Help button.

Help

The mouse pointer changes to an arrow with a question mark.

3 Click the Open text box.

A Help window appears, providing information on how to use the Open text box.

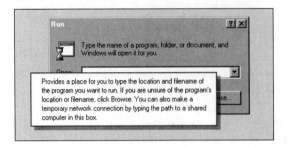

4 Click anywhere on the Desktop, or press ESC to close the Help window.

5 Click the Help button again, and then click Browse.

Help displays information about the Browse button.

6 Click Browse.

The Browse dialog box appears.

7 Click the Help button, and then click the Files Of Type list box.

The Help window appears with information about the list box.

8 Click Cancel.

9 In the Run dialog box, click Cancel.

 TIP You can change the way the Help topics appear on your screen. Click the Options button in the upper-right corner of any Help topic window, and then point to Font to change the font size.

Quitting Windows 95

To quit Windows 95 for now, you can follow these steps.

Quit Windows 95

1 Close all open windows by clicking the Close button in the upper-right corner of each window.

2 Click Start, and then click Shut Down.

3 When you see the message dialog box, click the Yes button.

 WARNING To avoid loss of data or damage to Windows 95, always quit Windows 95 using the Shut Down command on the Start menu before you turn your computer off.

Managing Your Files and Drives

Setting Up Your Computer

In this lesson you will learn how to:

■ Install additional Windows 95 components, and use Plug and Play devices.

■ Change the screen resolution for your computer.

■ Install the Easy Access options.

With Windows 95, it's easy to set up your computer to add new software and hardware. You can add a Windows 95 component, such as a screen saver or The Microsoft Network, that wasn't installed when you first set up Windows 95. If you want to see more information on your screen, you can change the screen resolution. You can also make Windows 95 easier to use by setting the Easy Access options. In this lesson, you'll learn how to install additional Windows 95 components and use Plug and Play, change your screen resolution, and set the Easy Access options.

Installing Additional Windows 95 Components

When you first install Windows 95, you choose the type of installation, such as Typical, Compact, Portable, or Custom. The type of installation you choose determines which Windows 95 components are installed. A *component* is a feature or accessory of Windows 95, such as the System Resource Monitor or Notepad. The components selected for each installation type are not the only components that you can install. Some components are installed by every installation type, but no installation option installs every component.

For example, as you set up Windows 95 for your home office, suppose you choose the Typical installation. The Typical installation includes many of the applications and settings you think you need to work with your files, your co-workers, and your customers. Suppose, however, that you find out that several of your customers want to communicate with you by using Windows 95 e-mail so that you can send and receive electronic messages using your phone line and a modem. You can install Microsoft Exchange and The Microsoft Network to work with e-mail. Or, you might purchase a new fax modem to replace a current modem that does not have faxing capability. After you install the fax modem, you would need to add software components to Windows 95 to take advantage of the features of your fax modem by installing the Microsoft Fax components for Microsoft Exchange.

Adding a Component

You can add a component to Windows 95 at any time. You might find it useful to know which components are installed during the setup of Windows 95. The following table describes the optional components installed for the Typical and Portable installation options in Windows 95. For Compact installation, no optional components are installed. For Custom installation, the Typical installation options are used, and you can select and confirm the components to install.

Optional component	Typical	Portable
Accessibility Options	•	—
Audio Compression	•	•
Backup	•	—
Briefcase	•	•
Calculator	•	•
CD Player	—	—
Character Map	—	—
Clipboard Viewer	—	—
Defrag	•	•
Desktop Wallpaper	—	—
Dial–Up Networking	—	•
Direct Cable Connection	—	•
Disk Compression Tools	—	•
Document Templates	•	—
Games	—	—
Hyper Terminal	•	•
Media Player	•	—
Microsoft Exchange	—	—

Optional component	Typical	Portable
Microsoft Fax	—	—
Microsoft Mail Services	—	—
Mouse Pointers	—	—
Net Watcher	—	—
Object Packager	•	—
Online User's Guide	—	—
Paint	•	—
Phone Dialer	•	•
Quick View	•	•
Screen Savers	•	•
Sound and Video Clips	—	—
Sound Recorder	—	—
System Monitor	—	—
The Microsoft Network	—	—
Video Compression	•	•
Volume Control	—	—
Windows 95 Tour	•	—
WordPad	•	—

These installation options select the components that most people will find useful. For example, the Typical installation option installs the components most useful for a typical office worker, while the Portable installation option installs components most useful on a portable computer. Sometimes you cannot install all of the components because your hard disk already has a large amount of data on it. In this case, you can add components after you erase some files or compress your hard disk. (Disk compression can squeeze more information in the same amount of disk space through a process of eliminating redundant information in files when they are stored on the disk. When you retrieve a file from a compressed disk, the redundant information is restored to the file.)

For example, you might have a large customer database file on your hard disk that leaves only about 10 MB of free disk space on your hard disk. Because Windows 95 needs between 20 to 40 MB of free disk space, you'll have to back up and then remove the database file from your hard disk to install Windows 95. After you've installed Windows 95 and compressed your disk, you can restore the database file to your hard disk. Even after you install Windows 95, you'll want to have at least 30 MB of free disk space available for the Windows swap file. The swap file is used by Windows 95 to move parts of programs or data back and forth (swap) from physical memory to disk. This technique makes it possible to run more and larger programs and use more and larger data files than can actually fit in the physical memory in your computer.

You use the Control Panel Add/Remove Programs icon to install additional components in Windows 95. Whether you choose to install Microsoft Exchange and The Microsoft Network components or the complete set of Windows 95 screen savers, the steps you take are basically the same.

To learn how to use the Add/Remove Programs icon, you'll install all of the screen savers that come with Windows 95—Flying Through Space, Mystify Your Mind, Curves and Colors, Scrolling Marquee, and Blank Screen.

Install an additional component

In this exercise, you install the remaining screen savers.

1   Click the Start button, point to Settings, and then click Control Panel.

2   In the Control Panel window, double-click the Add/Remove Programs icon.

3   In the Add/Remove Programs Properties dialog box, click the Windows Setup tab, and then click the word "Accessories."

   Don't click the check box next to Accessories—you'll select every accessory.

4   Click the Details button.

   The Accessories dialog box appears.

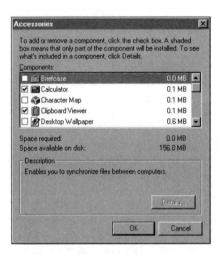

5   In the Accessories dialog box, scroll downward, and click the words "Screen Savers."

6   Click the Details button.

7   In the Screen Savers dialog box, click the check box for Additional Screen Savers, and then click OK.

8 Click OK, and then click OK again.

Windows Setup begins installing the additional screen savers.

9 If you're asked to insert a Windows 95 installation disk or Windows 95 Upgrade CD, insert the disk or CD, and then click OK.

10 On the Control Panel window, click the Close button.

Test the screen saver

1 Use the right mouse button to click the Desktop, and then click Properties.

2 Click the Screen Saver tab.

3 Click the Screen Saver down arrow, and then select Mystify Your Mind.

4 Click the Preview button.

The Mystify Your Mind screen saver starts.

5 Press any key to stop the screen saver, and then click the OK button.

You'll probably want to release the mouse after clicking Preview. Moving the mouse after the screen saver has started will stop the screen saver.

Removing a Component

You can remove a component as easily as you add one. Removing a component removes any information about the component. For example, if you remove all of the screen savers, you will no longer be able to use the Control Panel Display window to set a screen saver.

Removing a component removes the files used by the component. That is, if you remove the screen saver component, all the screen saver files (with a .SCR extension) are removed from your hard disk. If you want to reinstall the component, you must use the Windows 95 installation disk or CD to restore the screen saver files.

Suppose you decide you don't need the screen savers you installed and you want to remove them so that you can save disk space. After you delete the screen savers, however, you realize that you have no way to blank your screen when you leave your desk to run errands. You decide that the amount of disk space recovered isn't as important as the ability to blank your screen, so you will reinstall the screen savers.

 NOTE There are basically three reasons to use a screen saver. The first reason is to prevent image "burn-in," a condition that can result from displaying the same image on a monitor for an extended period of time. (Most contemporary monitors are not susceptible to image burn-in, so this doesn't apply to new systems.) The second reason is that screen savers provide a low level of security since they obscure what is currently displayed on the monitor. A screen saver can also incorporate the use of a password that is required to regain access to the computer. The third reason to use a screen saver is that they're really a lot of fun, providing another way to personalize your system.

Delete a screen saver

In this exercise, you delete the screen saver component. Later, you'll reinstall it.

1   Click the Start button, point to Settings, and then click Control Panel.

2   In the Control Panel window, double-click the Add/Remove Programs icon.

3   In the Add/Remove Programs Properties dialog box, click the Windows Setup tab, and then click the word "Accessories."

4   Click the Details button.

5   In the Accessories dialog box, scroll downward, and click the words "Screen Savers."

6   Click the Details button.

7   In the Screen Savers dialog box, remove the checkmark from Additional Screen Savers, and then click OK.

8   Click OK, and then click OK again.

9   On the Control Panel window, click the Close button.

Verify the screen saver is removed

1   Use the right mouse button to click the Desktop, and then click Properties.

2   On the Screen Saver tab, click the Screen Saver down arrow.

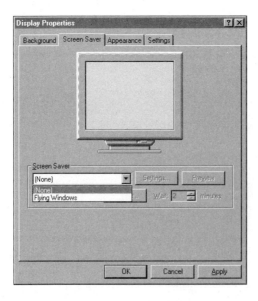

3   Verify that the Mystify Your Mind screen saver is removed.

4   Click the OK button.

Reinstall a screen saver

Suppose that you decide you want to use the screen saver you deleted after all. In this exercise, you reinstall the screen saver.

 Reinstall the screen saver by following the previous exercise, "Install an additional component."

Using Plug and Play

Plug and Play enables your computer to "sense" whenever a hardware device is attached to or removed from your computer. It was originally designed for computers (primarily laptops and small Desktop systems) that use *PC cards* (a Personal Computer Memory Card International Association, or PCMCIA, device) for optional accessories, such as network interface cards or modems. When you insert a modem PC card, Plug and Play immediately detects the presence of the new device and installs the appropriate drivers for the PC card. A driver is the software that Windows 95 (or any other operating system) uses to communicate with a device, such as a PC modem card. When you remove the modem PC card, Plug and Play detects that the card is no longer attached to your computer, removes the drivers from memory, and notifies any programs attempting to use the PC modem that the device is no longer available. The capability to attach and remove a device while your computer is running (hot) is called *hot swapping* or hot docking and it allows you to switch PC cards without rebooting your computer. Hot swapping is available only with a PCMCIA device.

Plug and Play capability is not limited to PCMCIA devices alone, however. Any Windows 95 computer system can make use of this capability. If you use Plug and Play compliant adapter cards, such as video, audio, disk, network, or modem cards, you will get most of the benefits of Plug and Play. If an adapter card supports (is compliant with) the Plug and Play standard, the product packaging will usually make this clear. Another component of Plug and Play is a part of your computer's system board, and is usually found only in newer systems. That component is called a Plug and Play BIOS (Basic Input Output System). If your system has such a BIOS, you will get the greatest ease of use and flexibility from Plug and Play. Typically, a computer that has a Plug and Play BIOS will display a message to that effect on the monitor when the computer is first turned on.

If you are adding a new device to your computer and it doesn't support Plug and Play, you can still install the drivers for the new device by using the Add Hardware icon in Control Panel.

The three levels of Plug and Play are as follows.

Cold Swapping The new device is only recognized when you restart the machine. This is the default mode for most Desktop computers and non-PCMCIA devices.

Warm Swapping The new device is recognized when you put the computer in sleep mode and then install the device. Laptops revert to sleep mode, a state where the screen is blanked and the hard disk is stopped from spinning, after a period of inactivity to preserve power. Most older laptops use this method to detect new PC cards.

Hot Swapping The new device is recognized whenever you insert the new card. Newer laptops use hot swapping Plug and Play.

Installing a New PC Card

Installing a PC card in a laptop computer is very easy: you just insert the PC card into the PCMCIA slot. You do not need to turn off your laptop computer. When you install new PCMCIA-compatible devices to a typical Desktop computer, however, you might need to turn the power off and insert the device, such as a modem or a SCSI card. After you've installed the PCMCIA-compatible device, you can turn it on. Depending on the configuration of your Desktop computer, it might immediately sense that the PC card has been installed.

Suppose, for example, that your home computer is a laptop computer with a docking station. You've decided to purchase a fax modem on a PC card, and you want to install it into your PCMCIA slot. You're not certain, however, what you need to do once you insert the PC card. You'll use the Plug and Play capability of Windows 95 to install the drivers for the PC card.

 NOTE This exercise assumes that you have a portable computer with a PCMCIA slot and a PC card available, and that the PCMCIA is set up to use the 32-bit PC Card Protected Mode Services. If you do not have these components available, and your computer is not set up with this service, skip to the section, "Customizing Your Startup Files."

Install the new PC card

In this exercise, you install a new device and then use Plug and Play to sense it.

1 If you have an older portable that doesn't support hot swapping, either turn it off or put it in sleep mode. If you have a newer portable, the PC card will be detected by the operating system.

2 Insert the PC card.

3 If you have an older portable that doesn't support hot swapping, either turn it back on or wake it up.

  The new PC card or device is automatically sensed by the operating system.

4 If this is the first time you've installed the device, you might be prompted to insert a Windows 95 installation disk or Windows 95 Upgrade CD. Insert the disk or CD, and then click OK.

Installing a New Device in a Desktop Computer

Suppose you have a new device that is not detected by Plug and Play. For example, your computer might not fully support Plug and Play, or the new device that you install might not be a Plug and Play device.

You can quickly install the drivers for the new device by using the Add New Hardware program in Control Panel. You first install the new device into your computer following the device manufacturer's recommendations. Then you start Windows 95 and run the Add New Hardware Wizard to install the drives for the device and configure it for use.

Install a new device

In this exercise, you install the drivers for a Microsoft Gameport Joystick. You can use these same steps to install other devices.

1 Click the Start button, point to Settings, and then click Control Panel.

2 In the Control Panel window, double-click the Add New Hardware icon.

The Add New Hardware Wizard starts to guide you through the hardware detection process.

If the device is automatically detected, you can still continue with the exercise by clicking No in step 3.

3 Click Next, and then click Yes to start a search for the new hardware device.

Your new device might be detected by Windows 95.

4 Click Next.

You are prompted that detecting the new hardware can take a few minutes. Also, you are reminded to close any other open programs.

5 Click Next again.

The detection process starts. After a few moments, the Add New Hardware Wizard finishes and prompts you to manually install the device.

6 Click Next. Scroll downward through the Hardware list, select Sound, Video, And Game Controllers, and then click Next.

The Add New Hardware Wizard displays a list of manufacturers and models.

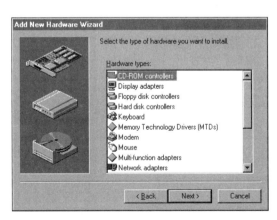

7 Scroll downward through the Manufacturer list and select Microsoft. In the Hardware list, select Gameport Joystick, and then click Next.

This is the new device you want to install.

8   If you're asked to insert a Windows 95 installation disk or Windows 95 Upgrade CD, insert the disk or CD, and then click OK.

The Add New Hardware Wizard displays resource settings for the new device.

9   Click Next, and then click Finish.

The new device is installed. You might be prompted to restart your machine to activate your new settings.

10   Click Restart.

Configuring a New Device

If you install a new device that is not detected by Plug and Play, you must manually configure it. Configuring a new device is usually straightforward. For example, suppose you connect a joystick to the gameport on the back of your computer. Before you can use the joystick, you must configure it. You might need to select the movement sensitivity for your joystick so that when you run Hover (a game that comes on the Windows 95 Upgrade CD), you do not continually run into the castle walls.

Configure a device

In this exercise, you configure the Microsoft Gameport Joystick you previously installed. If you do not have a Microsoft Gameport Joystick, and you are configuring another device, the Control Panel icon you use and the configuration method you use will be different.

1   Click the Start button, point to Settings, and then click Control Panel.

2   Double-click the Joystick icon.

3   Click the Calibrate button.

You are prompted to move the joystick in different directions to complete the test.

4   Click OK.

The test is complete.

5   On the Control Panel window, click the Close button.

Verifying the System Properties for Your Computer

When you set up a new device, you might accidentally make a mistake. For example, when you install a driver for a new Gameport Joystick, you might discover that the drivers for a joystick are already installed. You might also find that you have set up a modem to use some of the same settings as your mouse. A device conflict occurs whenever two or more devices, such as modems, video cards, or network interface cards, are configured to use the same system resources. A device conflict is similar to the phone company assigning your neighbor the same phone number that you have. Every time your phone rings, it might be for you or it might be for your neighbor. Whenever your devices receive a signal (phone call) to perform a function, they respond. Windows 95 will try to arbitrate device conflicts and disable devices that are trying to use system resources that have already been allocated to another device. If you are using Plug and Play devices, Windows 95 will try to automatically reconfigure the drivers so that they do not use the same resources.

You can identify and recover from device conflicts by examining the settings in the System Properties dialog box. You can also check other system settings, such as the resources used by a device or the drivers used by a device.

Check the settings for a device

In this exercise, you examine the settings for the Gameport Joystick you just installed. If you have installed another device, you can use these steps to check its settings.

You can also use the right mouse button to click My Computer on the Desktop and then click Properties on the shortcut menu.

1 Click the Start button, point to Settings, click the Control Panel, and then double-click the System icon.

2 Click the Device Manager tab.

3 Scroll downward, and click the plus sign (+) next to Sound, Video And Game Controllers.

A list of the devices under the Sound, Video And Game Controllers section appears. If there is a conflict in the device, a slashed circle appears over the device.

4 Click Gameport Joystick, and click the Properties button.

The Properties dialog box for the Gameport Joystick appears.

5 If there is a device conflict, click the check box next to Original Configuration (Current) to remove the checkmark. The device driver is disabled and the conflict is resolved.

You might need to remove the device entirely or double-check the information about the device before you reset the configuration.

If you receive an updated driver from your hardware manufacturer, click Change Driver, click Have Disk, and follow the prompts on screen to install the new driver.

6 Click the Driver tab.

A list of the drivers for the Gameport Joystick appears.

7 Click the Resources tab.

A list of the resources used by the Gameport Joystick appears.

8 Use the right mouse button to click Input/Output Range under Resource Settings, and then click What's This.

A brief explanation of the resource settings appears.

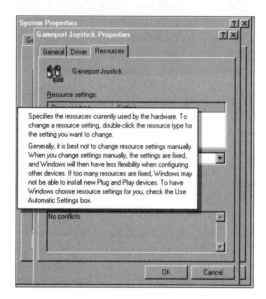

9 Click the Cancel button.

You don't want to make any changes right now to the properties for the Gameport Joystick. The Properties window closes.

10 Click the OK button.

The System window closes.

11 On the Control Panel window, click the Close button.

 NOTE You can also check your hardware device conflicts using the Hardware Troubleshooter in Windows 95 Help. Start Help, click the Index tab, type **troubleshooting, hardware conflicts**, and then click Display. Follow the steps in the Help dialog boxes to troubleshoot your device conflicts.

Changing Your Monitor Properties

Suppose you have several applications you want to use simultaneously, pasting information from one application to another. You can use the Tile Horizontally, Tile Vertically, or Cascade option on the taskbar to arrange the windows, but you'd like to be able to see more of the contents of the windows themselves.

You can modify the amount of information your screen displays by changing the *screen resolution*. The screen resolution determines the number of individual image elements per inch that are used to display the information on the monitor. A single image element is called a *picture element*, or *pixel*. The more pixels per inch, the finer the screen display on your monitor. The default screen display for VGA and Super VGA screens is 640 pixels wide by 480 tall. Most SVGA (Super VGA) screens support screen resolutions up to 1024 x 768, 1280 x 1024, or even 1600 x 1200 pixels.

For example, suppose the icons on the Desktop are 32 x 32 pixels. If you use a typical 14½-inch monitor running at 640 x 480 screen resolution, the icons are about ½ inch tall and wide. If you set the screen resolution to 1280 x 1024, the icons will be about ¼ inch tall and wide. The tradeoff for displaying more information is that some information might be too small to see without some adjustments.

You can also change the number of colors used to display information. The more colors your monitor can display per pixel, the better the images will look on your Desktop. Super VGA supports up to 256 colors per pixel. If your display adapter hardware supports it, you can also choose High Color (64 thousand colors per pixel) or True Color (16 million colors per pixel).

However, the more colors you choose per pixel, the longer it will take to redraw the screen when you make changes to a picture or when you switch from one program to another. The delay might not be noticeable if you have a very fast computer, but the delay might be annoying on a slower computer.

You can choose the resolution you want, switching from one to another, until you find the resolution that fits your needs.

Change the screen resolution

In this exercise, you select a different screen resolution. If you do not have a Super VGA monitor that supports higher screen resolution than 640 x 480, skip to the next exercise, "Change the number of colors."

You can also use the right mouse button to click the Desktop and then point to Properties.

1 Click the Start button, point to Settings, click Control Panel, and then double-click Display.

2 Click the Settings tab.

3 In the Desktop Area, drag the slider to the right to select 800 x 600 pixels.

If you cannot drag the slider, your monitor or display adapter card does not support higher resolutions.

4   If you are prompted to select a display monitor, click Change, click the manufacturer and model for your monitor, and then click OK.

5   Click the Font Size down arrow, and then click Large Fonts.

By selecting Large Fonts, the text used to identify information on your screen will be easier to read when you change your screen resolution.

6   Click OK.

7   If you are prompted to restart Windows, then click OK, and log on to Windows 95.

The screen resolution is changed.

 NOTE   Depending on the type of display adapter you have, you might be prompted to restart Windows 95 before the screen resolution can take effect.

You can easily change the number of colors used to display the information on your screen by selecting a color palette. A color palette controls the number of colors on your display. You can choose 16 colors, 256 colors, High Color (16-bit, 64 thousand colors), or True Color (24-bit, 16 million colors). You cannot choose a color palette that isn't supported by your monitor. If you don't like the number of colors you chose, you can reset your monitor back to the default. In most installations of Windows 95, the default is either 256 colors or 16 colors.

Change the number of colors

In this exercise, you change the number of colors used on your monitor. If you do not have a monitor that supports more than 256 colors, skip to the next section, "Installing the Easy Access Options."

1   Click the Start button, point to Settings, click Control Panel, and then double-click Display.

2   Click the Settings tab.

3   Click the Color Palette down arrow, and click High Color.

There is usually a trade-off between the number of colors and the total screen pixels your monitor can display. For example, setting your monitor resolution to 1024 x 768 pixels might only allow you to choose 16 or 256 colors.

4   Click OK.

5   If you are prompted to select a display monitor, click Change, select the manufacturer and model for your monitor, and then click OK. You also might be limited in the Font Size settings you can choose.

6 Click OK.

You are prompted to restart Windows 95.

7 Click OK, and log on to Windows 95.

The color palette is changed.

Installing the Easy Access Options

Suppose you work with Windows 95, but you have trouble using the mouse or keyboard. For example, you might not be able to hold down both CTRL and SHIFT simultaneously, or you might not be able to see the screen very well using the standard screen settings and colors.

You can adjust Windows 95 to meet your needs by changing the accessibility options. With the following options, you can change the features in Windows 95.

Accessibility tab	Options
Keyboard	**StickyKeys** allow you to press two keys sequentially rather than simultaneously. For example, instead of pressing and holding down ALT and then pressing the TAB key, you can press and release the ALT key and then press and release the TAB key to perform the same function.
	FilterKeys ignore unwanted, accidental keystrokes or repeated keystrokes. This will allow you to avoid a lot of retyping.
	ToggleKeys emit a tone through your computer's internal speaker whenever you press the CAPS LOCK key, the NUM LOCK key, or the SCROLL LOCK key. This alerts you that a key is active without looking at the keyboard.
Sound	**SoundSentry** creates a flash on your display whenever your computer generates a tone through its internal speaker. This alerts you that a tone is being generated if you can't hear the sound from the speaker.
	ShowSounds display information in a visual format that is normally presented in an audio format. Only certain programs support the use of ShowSounds.
Display	**HighContrast** changes your display settings to emphasize easy readability.
Mouse	**MouseKeys** will allow you to use the keys on the numeric keypad to move the mouse, click and double-click, and drag objects.

Accessibility tab	Options
General	**Automatic Reset** turns off all of the accessibility features after a specified idle period.
	Notification generates a tone or displays a message box or both whenever an accessibility option is turned on or off.
	SerialKey Devices allow you to use other hardware devices to perform the functions normally performed by the keyboard and mouse.

In the following exercises, you select the accessibility option so that your system makes a sound when you press the CAPS LOCK, the NUM LOCK, or the SCROLL LOCK key.

Change an accessibility option

1 Click the Start button, point to Settings, and then click Control Panel.

2 Double-click the Accessibility Option icon.

3 Click the check box next to Use Toggle Keys to place a checkmark in the box.

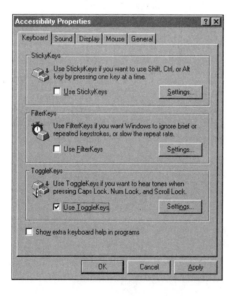

4 Click the Settings button next to Use Toggle Keys, click the check box next to Use Shortcut, and then click OK.

Selecting this option lets you toggle this accessibility feature by holding the NUM LOCK key for five seconds. That way, you don't have to open the Accessibility Option icon to turn the feature on or off.

5 Click OK.

Test the feature

It is not necessary to have a sound card to use this feature. The tones that you hear play through your PC speaker.

1 Press CAPS LOCK.

The CAPS LOCK key is turned on, and a tone sounds.

2 Press CAPS LOCK again.

The CAPS LOCK key is turned off, and a different, lower tone sounds.

3 Press and hold down the NUM LOCK key for at least five seconds.

The first tone you hear is to signify that the NUM LOCK key is turned on. After you wait five seconds, a different tone sounds to signify that the accessiblity option is turned off.

4 Press CAPS LOCK.

The CAPS LOCK key is turned on, but no tone sounds.

5 Press and hold down the NUM LOCK key for at least five seconds.

After five seconds, you are prompted to turn on the feature.

6 Click OK.

The accessibility feature is turned on.

7 Press CAPS LOCK.

The CAPS LOCK key is turned off, and a tone sounds.

One Step Further: Installing a New TrueType Font

Windows 95 comes with five default TrueType fonts: Arial, Courier New, Symbol, Times New Roman, and Wingdings. You might want to add more TrueType fonts to enhance your documents. You can get additional TrueType fonts from a variety of sources. Some applications, such as Microsoft Office, include TrueType fonts as part of the program. Or, you can purchase a separate TrueType pack. You install TrueType fonts using the Control Panel Font folder.

NOTE You can install a maximum of 1022 fonts. The actual number you can install on your own computer can vary because of the length of the font name and directory name used to store the fonts. However, you might want to limit the number of fonts you have installed, because Windows 95 works more quickly with fewer fonts installed. Also, the more fonts you have installed, the longer it takes to load a document. You also can use up to 1022 TrueType fonts in a single file.

Install a new font

Let's say that your corporate office has decided to produce documents that can be read by a document scanner. They've purchased a custom font, "Morse Code," and they want certain documents that are transmitted by fax to use this font. You've received a disk from the corporate office containing this font, and you must install it onto your computer. In this exercise, you install a new font from your Practice Files disk.

1   Insert the floppy disk into drive A or B.

2   Click the Start button, point to Settings, and then click Control Panel.

3   Double-click the Fonts icon.

4   On the File menu, click Install New Font.

5   Click the Drives down arrow, and then click drive A or B.

    A list of fonts on the drive appears.

6   In the List Of Fonts box, click Morse Code (TrueType).

7   Click OK.

8   On the Fonts window, click the Close button.

9   On the Control Panel window, click the Close button.

If you want to continue to the next lesson

1   Remove the Practice Files disk from drive A or B.

2   Close all open windows.

If you want to quit Windows 95 for now

1   Remove the practice files disk from drive A or B.

2   Close all open windows.

3   From the Start menu, click Shut Down, and then click Yes.

Lesson Summary

To	Do this
Install a new screen saver	Open the Control Panel. Open Add/Remove Programs. Click the Setup tab. Click Accessories, and then click the Details button. Scroll downward, and click Screen Savers. Click OK twice. Close the Control Panel window.
Remove a screen saver	Open the Control Panel. Open Add/Remove Programs. Click the Setup tab. Click Accessories, and then click the Details button. Scroll downward, and click the Screen Savers box to remove the checkmark. Click OK twice. Close the Control Panel window.
Install a new PC card	If necessary, turn off the computer. Then install the device. Turn the computer back on. When Windows 95 restarts, insert the Windows 95 disk or CD if needed.
Configure a new device	Open the Control Panel. Open the icon for the device. Click the appropriate tabs in the Properties window, and change the settings. Click Close. Close the Control Panel window.
Modify the screen resolution	Open the Control Panel. Open the Display icon. Click the Settings tab. Drag the Desktop Area slider bar to the resolution you want. Click OK. If necessary, restart Windows 95.
Modify the color palette	Open the Control Panel. Open the Display icon. Click the Settings tab. Click the Color Palette down arrow, and click the color palette you want. Click OK. If necessary, restart Windows 95.
Modify the Accessibility Options	Open the Control Panel. Click the Accessibility Options icon. Click the tab for the item you want to change, and then click the option you want. Click OK.

For online information about	From the Help dialog box, click Index and then type
Installing and removing Windows 95 components	**installing, Windows components**
Installing new devices	**installing, hardware**
Verifying system properties	**system properties, viewing**
Changing screen resolution	**screen, resolution changing**
Installing Easy Access options	**installing, accessibility options**

Preview of the Next Lesson

In the next lesson, you'll learn how to add programs to your StartUp folder so that the programs you use start when Windows 95 starts. You'll learn to modify your computer settings so that multiple users can use your computer without changing the settings for other users. And, you'll learn how to change the system policies for specific users, so you can modify the access each user has to specific features of Windows 95.

Customizing Windows 95 for Multiple Users

Estimated time

40 min.

In this lesson you will learn how to:

- Customize your startup files.
- Set up your computer for multiple users.
- Modify the system policies for your computer.

Suppose you share your computer with one or more users. Each user would like to have a different Windows 95 work environment, such as a customized StartUp folder that opens specific programs or files only when that user logs on. For security reasons, you also might want to restrict the activities of certain users so that, for example, they cannot view network settings or change the settings in the Control Panel. In this lesson, you'll learn how to customize your own startup files, add multiple users to your computer, and create individualized system policy restrictions.

Customizing Your StartUp Folder

You might find that as you work through your day that you have several programs or files that you use frequently. For example, imagine that in your home office you must keep a daily log of your work duties to turn in to your manager every month. Each morning when you turn on your computer, you open your logbook file in Windows 95 and use it during the day to keep track of your activities. Rather than manually opening the logbook file each day, you can have Windows 95 automatically open it by placing the logbook file in the StartUp folder. That way, whenever you start Windows 95, the logbook will open.

23

NOTE   You can drag any program or file or its shortcut into the StartUp folder. It is recommended that you place shortcuts for programs, rather than the program files themselves in the StartUp folder, because some programs don't work properly if they're moved from their original folder location.

Modify the contents of the StartUp folder

In this exercise, you create a new document in the StartUp folder that automatically opens each time you start Windows 95.

1   Use the right mouse button to click the Start button, and then click Open.

2   Double-click the Programs icon, and then double-click the StartUp folder icon.

3   Use the right mouse button to click in the StartUp window. On the shortcut menu, point to New, and then click Text Document.

   A new text document is created.

4   Make sure the name "New Text document" is selected, type **Daily Log,** and press ENTER.

5   Double-click the Daily Log icon.

   The new Daily Log text document opens in Notepad.

6   Type **This is my Daily Log for today** and press ENTER twice.

7   On the File menu, click Save.

8   Click the Close button.

9   Hold down the SHIFT key and click the Close button on the StartUp window.

   Holding down SHIFT when you click the Close button closes the current window and any of the windows you opened to get to the current window.

Test the StartUp folder

Now that you've placed the logbook file into the StartUp folder, you can test it. When you restart Windows 95, you will see the logbook open on the Desktop.

1   Click the Start button, and then click Shut Down.

2   Click Restart The Computer, and then click OK.

3   Log on to Windows 95 by using your usual identification and password.

   After your identification and password are accepted, Windows 95 starts. The Daily Log text document opens.

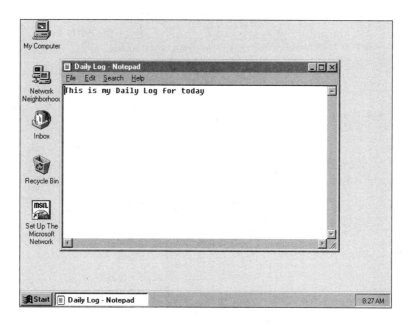

4   Press CTRL+END, type **Today I'm customizing Windows 95**, and then press ENTER twice.

5   On the File menu, click Save.

6   On the Daily Log window, click the Close button.

   TIP   Usually, when Windows 95 starts, the items in the StartUp folder are opened. If you want to bypass the items in the StartUp folder, you can hold down F8 during the startup of Windows 95 to see a menu of startup options from which you can select. To bypass just the items in the StartUp folder when Windows 95 starts, enter your identification and password at the prompts, and then hold down the CTRL or SHIFT key.

Setting Up Your Computer for Multiple Users

Suppose the computer in your home office is set up to open your log file when you start Windows 95. However, when you are out of the office, your assistant doesn't want to see your log file when he uses your computer.

You can use Windows 95 to set up multiple *user profiles* on the same machine. A user profile is a collection of settings that are specific to each user. For example, you could have one setting for yourself that opens the log file and another setting for your assistant that does not open the log file. By enabling multiple user profiles, each user who logs on to Windows 95 at your workstation can keep his or her settings separate.

Setting the Defaults for All Users

Before you set up multiple user profiles, it's a good idea to make your workstation setup as simple as possible. When you enable multiple user profiles, the current Windows 95 settings, including the Control Panel settings and the contents of the StartUp folder, become the default settings for all users. When setting defaults for multiple users, config- ure your system with the settings that everyone will most likely use—don't spend a lot of time configuring default settings for things that will likely get changed by each user. For example, most users would probably benefit from having a shortcut to a network printer placed on their Desktop, whereas, most users will want to personalize their screen savers and colors. After you've simplified your Windows 95 startup and enabled multiple user profiles, each user can then log on and customize Windows 95 for his or her own use.

In the following exercises, you'll first establish standard settings for multiple user profiles. Then you'll modify your own profile and verify that other users' profiles are not affected. Finally, you'll set your computer back to the normal single-user mode.

Set the default settings

In this exercise, you'll simplify your setup by removing the daily log file from the StartUp folder. You'll leave all the other settings as they are.

1 Use the right mouse button to click Start, and then click Open.
2 Double-click Programs, and then double-click StartUp.
3 Use the right mouse button to click Daily Log, and then click Delete.
4 Click Yes, and then click the Close button on all open windows.

Enable multiple user profiles

After you've selected the Windows 95 settings you want for all users, you can enable multiple user profiles.

1 Click Start, point to Settings, and then click Control Panel.
2 Double-click Passwords, and then click the User Profiles tab.

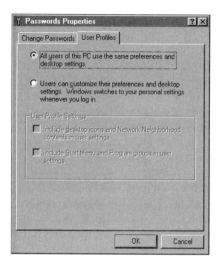

3 Click the second option button to customize preferences.

4 Click Include Start Menu And Program Groups In User Settings to place a checkmark in the check box.

5 Click OK.

6 Click Yes to restart your computer.

Log on as yourself

1 When the computer restarts, log on with your user identification and password.

You might be prompted to confirm your user identification and password if you've never used multiple passwords and user profiles on your computer.

2 Windows 95 starts with the default settings.

Change the Desktop

In this exercise, you'll change your Desktop settings to verify that multiple user profiles are selected.

1 Use the right mouse button to click the Desktop, and then click Properties.

2 Click the Background tab.

3 In the Wallpaper list, click Arcade, click the Tile option, and then click OK.

When you shut down Windows 95, these settings will be retained and used the next time you log onto Windows 95 at your workstation.

Log on as another user

In this exercise, you'll log on as Pat Lee and make changes to the Windows 95 settings.

1   Click Start, click Shut Down, click Close All Programs And Log On As A Different User, and then click OK.

2   When Windows 95 restarts, log on as Pat Lee (your assistant). Use the user identification **plee** and the password **helper**.

3   If you are asked to confirm you password, type the password in the logon window, and then click OK.

4   Click Yes to retain settings for the next time you log on to this computer.

    Pat Lee's settings are the same as the default settings for Windows 95.

Now both yourself and Pat Lee can customize the Desktop for Windows 95 and not affect each other's settings.

Log on as yourself

1   Click Start, click Shut Down, click Close All Programs And Log On As A Different User, and then click OK.

2   When the computer restarts, log on with your user identification and password.

Verifying the System Policies

Suppose that you have several users working on your home office computer. You are confident that each person can modify Windows 95 to his or her needs, but you don't want anyone to make adjustments to critical information, such as which network server is accessed by a workstation.

You can control what changes a user can make by modifying the system policies for your workstations. The system policies control what changes a user can make on the system. To use system policies, you must enable user profiles. To modify the system policies, you use the System Policy Editor, an optional component of Windows 95 that is only available on the CD-ROM version of Windows 95.

When you modify any system policy, you can choose between three options:

Option	Definition	Symbol
Enable	The property is enabled when the user logs on. The user will be able to perform the function that is enabled.	☑
Disable	The property is disabled when the user logs on. The user will not be able to perform the function that is specifically disabled.	☐

Option	Definition	Symbol
Ignore	The property is bypassed when the user logs on. It is neither enabled nor disabled. Windows 95 starts more quickly if you leave most properties set to this option.	

In the next exercises, you install the System Policy editor, modify a few policies, test them, and then reset them. If you do not have access to the Windows 95 CD-ROM, skip to the One Step Further exercise at the end of the lesson.

> **NOTE** When you insert the Windows 95 CD-ROM, the AutoPlay feature opens the Autorun.exe program. Holding down SHIFT while you insert a CD-ROM into your CD-ROM drive bypasses the AutoPlay feature.

Install the System Policy Editor

In this exercise, you install the System Policy Editor.

1 Hold down SHIFT, and then insert the Windows 95 CD-ROM into your CD-ROM drive.

2 Click the Start button, point to Settings, and click Control Panel.

3 Double-click the Add/Remove Programs icon, and then click the Windows Setup tab.

4 Click the Have Disk button, and then click the Browse button.

5 In the Drives area, select your CD-ROM drive.

6 Verify that the path is set to admin\apptools\poledit, click OK, and then click OK again.

   The dialog box displays the two features of the System Policy Editor. You will select them both.

7 Click the check box next to System Policy Editor and the Group policies options.

8 Click Install.

   Windows 95 installs the System Policy Editor and group-based support for system policies.

9 Click OK, and then, on the Control Panel window, click the Close button.

Select the policy template

In this exercise, you select the policy template that you will be using for the remainder of the exercises in this lesson.

1 Click the Start button, point to Programs, point to Accessories, point to System Tools, and click System Policy Editor.

2 On the Options menu, click Template.

You must first select the file containing the master settings before you can modify the current settings.

3 If the active template is not ADMIN.ADM, click the Open Template button. In the File Name box, type **c:\windows\inf\admin.adm** and then click Open.

The admin.adm file is copied to the inf directory when you install the System Policy Editor.

4 Click the Close button.

Modify the system policies for a user

In this exercise, you create a system policy file and specify a restriction for a specific user.

1 On the File menu, click New File.

A new set of settings is created.

2 On the toolbar, click Add User.

Add User

You can also click Add User on the Edit menu.

3 In the Type The Name Of The User To Add box, type **plee** and then click OK.

A new user icon is created for Pat Lee.

4 Double-click the Plee icon (the user icon for Pat Lee).

The Plee Properties window opens.

5 Click the plus sign next to System.

6 Click the plus sign next to Restrictions.

The Restrictions for Plee appear.

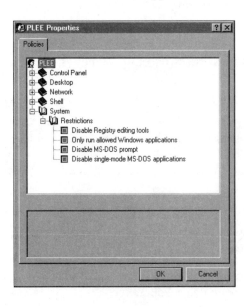

7   Click the check box next to Disable Registry Editing Tools to enable the option.

When this check box is checked, the option is turned on, so Pat Lee cannot edit the registry (the collection of system settings for Windows 95). If you click the check box three times, the check box is colored gray, and the option will be ignored when Windows 95 starts. Windows 95 will simply use the previous setting, which saves time when you start up.

8   Click OK.

Modify the system policies for the computer

In this exercise, you change the policy for your computer. Computer policies are always in effect for all users of the computer.

 ⚠ WARNING   After you have created a policy that applies to a specific user, be careful if you change settings for any of the policy options. You could permanently lose that user's settings.

1   Double-click the Default Computer icon.

2   Click the plus sign next to Network, and then click the plus sign next to Logon.

3   Click the check box next to Logon Banner to place a checkmark in the check box.

Setting this option displays a message box before Windows 95 starts, warning all users that they must use a valid user identification and a valid password to access the computer.

4   Scroll downward, and click the plus sign next to System.

5   Click the check box next to Enable User Profiles to place a checkmark in the check box.

Setting this option enables user profiles.

6   Click OK.

Save the system policies

1   On the File menu, click Save.

2   In the File Name box, type **c:\config.pol**

The system policies are usually in a file called config.pol.

3   Click OK.

Specify the system policy file to use at startup

Normally, Windows 95 will look in a specific, default folder on a network server for the system policy file to use at startup. In your home office, you don't have a Novell Netware or Windows NT server, so you'll need to change where Windows 95 looks for the system policy file.

31

1   On the File menu, click Open Registry.

2   Double-click the icon for Local Computer.

3   Click the plus sign next to Network, and then click the plus sign next to Update.

4   Click the text Remote Update, and then in the Update Mode text box, click the down arrow and click Manual (Use Specific Path).

5   In the Path For Manual Update box, type **c:\config.pol**

6   Click OK and then click Save on the File menu.

7   On the File menu, click Exit.

Test the new system policy

1   Click Start, click Shut Down, click Restart The Computer, and then click Yes.

    When the computer restarts, a logon banner appears.

2   Click OK.

3   When the logon window appears, sign on as **plee** (Pat Lee), and type the password **helper**

4   Click the Start button, click Run, type **regedit** in the Run box, and then click OK.

    A dialog box appears, warning you that your ability to edit the registry has been denied by the administrator.

5   Click OK.

TIP   To reset the system policies for a user, start the System Policy Editor, select the icon for the user that you want to reset, and then click Remove on the Edit menu. Make sure you have not altered the settings for the default user, since those settings will be used the next time that user logs on to the system.

Revert to your normal log on procedure

In this exercise, you'll restore your system to have a single profile for all users.

NOTE   If you are going to do the One Step Further exercise at the end of this lesson, skip this exercise for now.

---

1   Click Start, point to Settings, and click Control Panel.

2   Open Passwords, and then click the User Profiles tab.

3   Click All Users Of The PC Use The Same Preferences And Desktop Settings.

4   Click Include Start Menu And Program Groups In User Settings to remove the checkmark in the check box, and then click OK.

5   Click Yes to restart your computer.

6   When Windows 95 restarts, log in as yourself.

One Step Further: Restricting Access to Programs

By default, Windows 95 can run any program installed on your computer. You can restrict access to programs, however, if you want to keep users from running unauthorized programs.

Restrict program access

Let's say that your corporate office has decided that unauthorized users cannot run any programs except for the installed Office suite. You can modify the access list in the System Policy Editor so that no one can run any other program.

1   Click the Start button, point to Programs, point to Accessories, point to System Tools, and click System Policy Editor.

2   Double-click the Plee icon, click the plus sign next to System, and then click the plus sign next to Restrictions.

3   Click the check box next to Only Run Allowed Windows Applications to place a checkmark in the check box.

4   Click the Show button, and then click the Add button.

5   In the Type Name Of The Program To Be Added box, type **WordPad.exe** and then click OK.

You can type the name of whatever program to which you want to allow access, but remember that any program that is not in this list will not be accessible to Pat Lee. The programs in this list are the only programs that Pat Lee can run.

6   Click OK, and then click OK again.

7   On the File menu, click Save.

8   On the System Policy Editor window, click the Close button.

9   Log on as Pat Lee and test the new policy and then log on again using your normal user identification and password.

10 Return to and complete the previous exercise, "Revert to your normal log on procedure."

If you want to continue to the next lesson

➤ Close all open windows.

If you want to quit Windows 95 for now

1 Close all open windows.
2 On the Start menu, click Shut Down. Then click Yes.

Lesson Summary

To	Do this
Customize the StartUp folder	Open the StartUp folder. Drag icons to the StartUp folder, or create a new file. Close the StartUp folder, and restart Windows.
Set up your computer for multiple users	Open the Control Panel. Open Passwords, and then click the User Profiles tab. Click Users Can Customize Their Preferences And Desktop Settings. Click the Start Menu And Program Groups In User Settings if it is not selected. Click OK, and then click Yes to restart your computer.
Modify the system policies for a user	Open the System Policy Editor. On the File menu, click New File. Click the Add User icon, type a name for the new user, and then click OK. Double-click the new user icon. Modify the settings, and then click OK.

To	Do this
Modify the system policies for a computer	Click the Add Computer icon, type a name for the computer, and then click OK. Modify the settings, and then click OK.
Save the system policies	On the File menu, click Save As. In the File Name box, type **c:\config.pol** and then click Save.
Specify the system policy file to use at startup	On the File menu click Open Registry. Double-click Local Computer, double-click Update. Change the update mode to manual and specify a path of C:\config.pol in the Path For Manual Update box. Click OK. On the System Policy Editor window, click the Close button.

For online information about	From the Help dialog box, click Index and then type
Customizing your system startup	**StartUp folder, adding programs to**
Configuring multiple users	**setting up, customized settings for multiple users**
System policies	**new policy file, creating** (from the System Policy Editor Help dialog box, on the Index tab)

Preview of the Next Lesson

In the next lesson, you'll learn about managing your hard disk. You'll back up and restore files, find and fix common disk problems, optimize your disks, and compress your hard disk.

Managing Your Hard Disk

Lesson 3

In this lesson you will learn how to:

- Back up and restore files to your hard disk.
- Find and fix common disk problems.
- Optimize your hard disk.
- Compress your hard disk.

Estimated time
40 min.

With Windows 95, it's easy to perform routine maintenance on your hard disk. You can use the tools in Windows 95 to back up your files to a backup disk and then restore them when you want to use the information again. You can use the disk management tools to find and fix common disk problems, or make your hard disk work more efficiently by using Disk Defragmenter to optimize your files. You can also double the amount of disk storage space that you have available using the tools in Windows 95. In this lesson, you'll manage your hard disk by backing up and restoring files, fixing common disk problems, and optimizing and compressing your hard disk.

Backing Up and Restoring Your Hard Disk

The data on your hard disk is a valuable asset representing many hours of time and effort. Even though hard disks infrequently fail, they are mechanical devices and as such they *will* fail eventually. When they do fail, the results are often catastrophic. For example, should your hard disk fail, you might lose the only copy of a customer list or an accounts receivable file. It's a good idea, therefore, to *back up* critical data frequently. You back up your data by copying it to another disk, to a backup tape, or to some other kind

37

of removable media that can store a large amount of information. When you back up your data, you store all the files and folder in one large file. The data in the backup file is compressed, so you can save space on the backup medium.

Let's say in your home office, you store your customer invoicing information on the computer used by your part-time assistant, Pat Lee. Every few days, he enters customer transactions for you. Imagine what might happen if the computer failed to start one morning. Unless you had the data backed up, you might lose valuable and irreplaceable information that could cost your business a lot of time and money.

Considering Backup Strategies

Suppose you have critical data that you want to back up frequently. You can back up your data to a tape cartridge or to disk each day, but suppose your backup medium is also somehow damaged.

It's a good idea to develop a backup strategy in which you back up your files on a frequent basis to different media. For example, suppose you back up your hard disk every Wednes-day afternoon to your tape cartridge. Then, each Monday and Friday afternoon, you can back up selected files to a set of disks. On Monday, you might back up selected files to one set of disks, then, on Friday, you might back up selected files to another set of disks.

If you have a disk crash on Tuesday, you can use the Wednesday backup tape cartridge to restore your computer, then you can use the Monday backup disks to restore the files that were modified since the Wednesday backup.

Weekly backup to high-capacity removable media

Twice weekly backup of selected files to disk

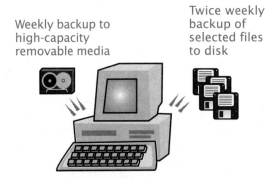

By rotating the resource you use to store your backup files, you reduce the risk of losing your data.

Installing the Backup Program

You can use the Backup program in Windows 95 to back up and restore your data files. You can back up your entire hard disk, selected folders, selected files, or both selected folders and files.

If you have a tape drive, optical disc drive, or cartridge drive, you can use it to store the files. These devices are designed to store large amounts of data. Also, these drives usually make it easy to find a backup file or folder so that you can restore it. Because you can store the tape, disk, or cartridge in another location, such as a safe deposit box or a locked file cabinet, you can protect against losing data that might occur if your computer is damaged or unusable. If you do not have one of these devices, you can use another hard disk, a floppy disk, or a network folder as a backup location. However, hard disks and network folders are difficult to physically transfer to another location, and floppy disks do not hold much information. .

Imagine that you have recently purchased and installed a tape drive on your home office computer. You want to use the tape drive to back up the critical files on your hard disk. After you've backed up your hard disk onto the tape cartridge, you'll take the cartridge and store it in a safe place.

Because Backup is an optional component of Windows 95, you must install the Backup program before you use it.

Install Backup

In this exercise, you install the Backup program from the Windows setup disks or CD. If you've already installed Backup, you can skip this exercise.

1   Click Start, point to Settings, and then click Control Panel.

2   In the Control Panel window, double-click the Add/Remove Programs icon.

3   In the Add/Remove Programs Properties dialog box, click the Windows Setup tab.

4   In the Windows Setup tab window, select the Disk Tools option, and then click the Details button.

   The Disk Tools dialog box appears.

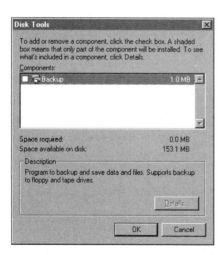

5   Select the Backup component option.

   A checkmark appears in the Backup component check box.

6 Click OK, and then click OK again.

Windows Setup begins installing the Backup component. You might be asked to insert a disk or CD to complete the process.

7 On the Control Panel folder window, click the Close button.

Backing Up Your Hard Disk

To use the Backup program to back up your disk, you need to perform the following steps:

- Start the Backup program.
- Select the item or items you want to back up.
- Start backing up the files.

If you back up the same items frequently, you can name and save a *backup set* so that you can use it again to back up the same items. A backup set is a file that stores your backup settings, such as the names of the files and folders you want to back up. By using a named backup set, you can save yourself the time it takes to specify the files and folders you want to back up.

For example, each week you might want to back up your customer accounts, which are stored in a folder called Customer Accounts. You can mark the Customer Accounts folder in the Backup window so that it is backed up, and then save the backup set with the name Customer Accounts Weekly Backup. Each Friday afternoon, you can start Backup, open the Customer Accounts Weekly Backup backup set, and then proceed to perform the backup.

Start Backup

If you do not have a tape backup device, you can still perform this exercise by using a blank formatted disk as your backup location.

In the More Windows SBS Practice folder you have a folder called Storage. Imagine that you would like to regularly back up this folder. In this exercise, you start Backup and begin backing up the Storage folder.

NOTE When you run Backup, it will check to see if there is a tape drive in your system. If Backup cannot find a tape drive, a dialog box will appear asking you to confirm that you do not have a tape drive. Click OK if your computer does not have a tape drive. If your computer does have a tape drive, read the information in the dialog box for some useful tips.

1 Insert a tape cartridge in the tape drive.

If you want to use a floppy disk to store your backup file, insert a blank, formatted floppy disk into drive A or B. (Do not use the Practice Files disk that came with this book.)

2 Click Start, point to Programs, point to Accessories, point to System Tools, and then click Backup.

*If you see the
Welcome To
Microsoft
Backup dialog
box, click OK.*

3 Click OK.

The Initializing Microsoft Backup window appears. Backup checks the installed hardware to determine whether the tape drive and tape cartridge are installed and available. After a few moments, the window closes and the Microsoft Backup window appears, reminding you that a full system backup set was created.

4 Read the text in the dialog box to learn more about a full system backup, and then click OK.

The Untitled - Microsoft Backup application window appears.

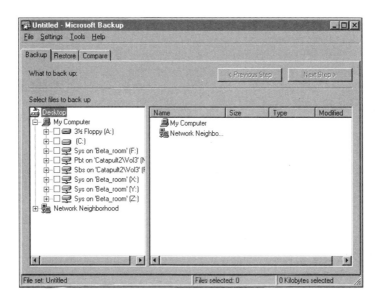

Select the folder to back up

Unless you want to back up your entire hard disk, it's a good idea to select only specific folders or files you want to back up. For example, you could back up the entire disk on your home office computer to a tape drive, but it would take a long time and would probably require several tape cartridges. Instead, it would be more efficient to back up only critical data, because you can always reinstall programs from their installation disks.

In this exercise, you select the Storage folder as the folder you want to back up.

1 In the Microsoft Backup window, click the plus sign (+) next to the drive C icon.

The list of folders on drive C appears.

2 Click the plus sign next to the More Windows SBS Practice folder.

The list of folders in the More Windows SBS Practice folder appears.

3 Click the check box next to the Storage folder.

All the files in the Storage folder are selected.

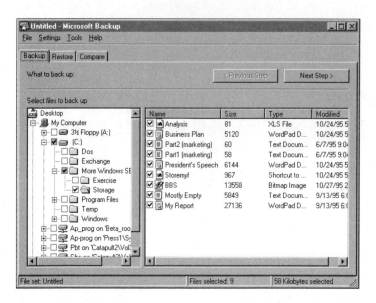

4 Click the Next Step button.

The Microsoft Backup window displays a list of available destinations.

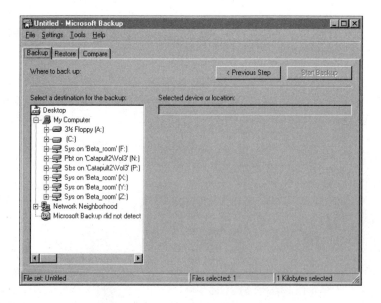

If you do not have a tape drive, you can use drive A or B as the backup device.

5   Scroll downward in the Select A Destination For Backup list until you see a tape drive icon.

   If you do not see a tape drive icon, on the Tools menu click Redetect Tape Drive. If you still do not see a tape icon, check to be sure that the tape cartridge is inserted in the tape drive correctly.

6   Select the tape drive icon.

   The tape drive is selected as the location to which your files will be backed up.

Save the backup file set

Now that you've selected the folder and the backup location, you can save the backup settings with the name Storage Backup. That way, you can back up the same folder each week by opening the named backup set.

1   On the File menu, click Save As.

2   In the File Name box, select the text "Full System Backup" and type **Storage Backup**

3   Click the Save button.

Start the backup

You can drag the backup set file to the Backup icon to start backing up files.

1   Click the Start Backup button.

2   In the Backup Set box, type **Storage Backup**

3   Click OK.

   When the backup is complete, a message box appears with the text "Operation Complete."

4   In the message box, click OK, and then click OK again.

5   Click the Close button on Microsoft Backup.

Now that you've backed up the Storage folder to the tape cartridge, you can put the tape cartridge in a safe location.

Restoring Your Hard Disk

Suppose you've been backing up your hard disk regularly. Each Friday afternoon, your assistant backs up the Storage folder to your tape drive. One Monday morning, you turn on the computer and open the Storage folder, but you notice that the files are missing. You ask your assistant, who tells you he is sure he didn't delete the files. The Recycle Bin is empty, and you don't have a copy of the folder handy. But you remember the weekly backups, so you can get the tape cartridge and use it to restore the files that are missing.

In the following exercises, you'll restore the Storage folder. To emulate this scenario, you'll first delete the Storage folder and then restore the folder from your tape cartridge.

Delete the Storage folder

 ⚠ **WARNING**   Before completing this step, review the contents of the Recycle Bin. Emptying Recycle Bin deletes its entire contents.

1   Drag the Storage folder from the More Windows SBS Practice folder to the Recycle Bin.

2   Use the right mouse button to click the Recycle Bin.

3   On the shortcut menu, click Empty Recycle Bin, and then click Yes.

The contents of Recycle Bin are purged. You cannot recover purged files.

Start Backup

1   Insert the tape cartridge containing the Storage Backup set into the tape drive (or insert the floppy disk into the disk drive).

2   Click Start, point to Programs, point to Accessories, point to System Tools, and then click Backup.

If you see the Welcome to Microsoft Backup dialog box, click OK.

3   Click OK.

4   Click the Restore tab.

5   In the Restore From area, scroll downward in the list and select the tape drive icon (or the disk drive icon).

6   Click Storage Backup.

Start restoring the files

1   Click the Next Step button.

Backup begins searching the backup tape for the Storage Backup files. After a few moments, the drive C icon appears in the Contents Of "Storage Backup" list.

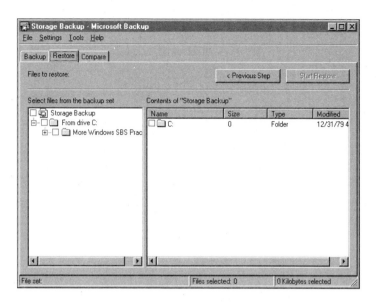

2   Click the plus sign next to the From Drive C folder icon.

The list of folders in the From Drive C folder appears.

3   Click the plus sign next to the More Windows SBS Practice folder icon.

The list of folders in the More Windows SBS Practice folder appears.

4   Click the Storage folder icon.

A list of files available for restoration appears in the Contents Of "Storage" window.

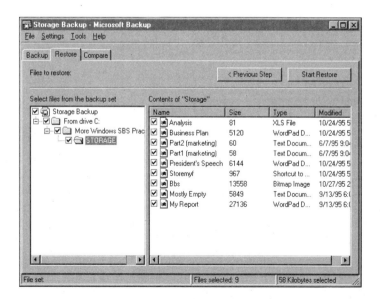

5   Click the check box next to the Storage folder icon.

The files in the Storage folder are selected.

6   Click the Start Restore button.

The restoration process starts. After a few moments, the restoration process ends and a message box appears.

7   In the message box, click OK, and then click OK again.

8   On the Untitled - Microsoft Backup window, click the Close button.

Verify the contents of the Storage folder

Now that you've restored the Storage folder, you can check to see that the files were restored correctly. In this exercise, you open the Storage folder and examine its contents.

1   Use My Computer to find and open the Storage folder.

The folder opens, displaying its contents.

2   Verify that there are nine files in the Storage folder. Then, on the Storage window, click the Close button.

Finding and Fixing Common Disk Problems

Your personal computer is a dependable tool for productivity and organization. However, it's inevitable that problems will occur with your hardware. For example, your computer might suffer a hard disk crash (extremely serious and beyond the scope of this book to repair) or, more commonly, there might be physical damage to the disk or to a file resulting in missing information.

Understanding Common Causes of Disk Problems

As shown in the following illustration, the surface of a disk is divided into *tracks* (concentric circles that start at the center of the disk and go outward). Tracks are divided into *sectors.* Each sector stores the same amount of information, typically 512 bytes. A *cluster,* which consists of a group of sectors, is the smallest unit used for storing a file or a part of a file. The size of a cluster varies with the size of the entire disk. The larger the total capacity of a disk, the larger the size of its clusters. All the clusters on any one disk, however, are the same size. A file can be any size, up to the limits of the operating system. When you save a file, it is stored in the first available cluster. When that cluster is filled, the remainder of the file is stored in the next available clusters on the disk.

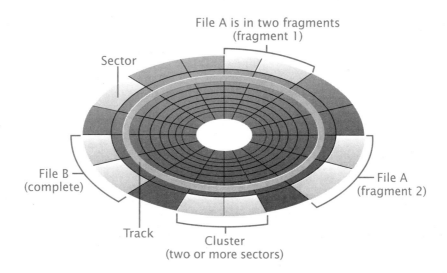

File A is in two fragments
(fragment 1)

Sector

File B
(complete)

File A
(fragment 2)

Track

Cluster
(two or more sectors)

Bad Sectors A *bad sector* is any sector on a disk that is not capable of storing information. A bad sector is frequently the result of a defect in a physical area of a disk that renders the sector unusable for storing data. It might result from a manufacturing flaw, a worn-out area, or possibly from sharply bumping the computer while it is writing to the hard disk. Although the area on the disk that is occupied by the bad sector might have some permanent damage, the remaining sectors on the hard disk are usually undamaged. Repairing the damage requires that the computer's operating system mark the damaged sector as unusable, so that no data will be written to that sector in the future.

Any data in the damaged area is probably irretrievable, but the remainder of the hard disk can be used without fear of future problems. If you do not have the operating system mark bad sectors as unusable, however, any information that is stored on that portion of the hard disk will be unreliable. By marking the bad sector, you ensure that the data stored on your hard disk is reliable.

TROUBLESHOOTING   A bad sector located in the boot sector of your hard disk makes your hard disk unbootable. The *boot sector* is a specific disk sector that your computer uses to start Windows 95. You can still use the damaged hard disk as a secondary hard disk (such as drive D). You'll then need to replace the unbootable hard disk with a new, bootable hard disk.

Lost Clusters As mentioned earlier, your computer stores each file on your disk in units called clusters. Although the multiple clusters for a given file might not all be physically adjacent on the disk, the operating system keeps track of which of these *file fragments* contains the beginning of the file, the end of the file, and the middle pieces of the file, in sequence. Under certain circumstances, such as a sudden loss of power or a program unexpectedly freezing in mid-operation, only part of a file might be stored on the disk. Such partial file fragments, which are not associated with complete files, take up space on the disk, occupying what are called *lost clusters*.

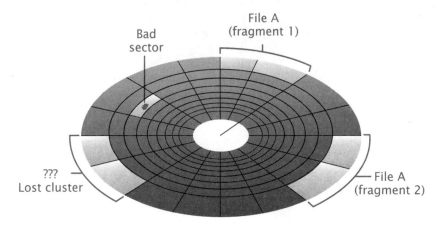

If you do not locate and remove lost clusters, no damage is done to your disk or files. However, because the space is marked as used, Windows 95 will not use the space for any other files. The space cannot be recovered by erasing any file, because the information is not part of a file. The more lost clusters you have, the less disk space you'll have for other files. Recovering the space used by lost clusters gives you more space to store files on your hard disk.

Repairing this problem involves having the computer either convert each lost cluster into a complete file or convert the lost clusters into files and then immediately erase the files. Usually erasing is the best option, because the information in a lost cluster is often unreliable anyway.

Lost clusters are not a common problem, especially if you use the Shut Down command before you turn off your computer. If you have a program that regularly freezes so that you must use CTRL+ALT+DELETE to close it, you should contact the manufacturer for an updated version that runs well under Windows 95.

Fixing Disk Problems with ScanDisk

Windows 95 includes ScanDisk, a program that can help find and fix common disk errors. By default, ScanDisk is installed when you install Windows 95. After you start ScanDisk, you can set several configuration options. You can choose the default settings, or you can adjust the operation of ScanDisk. For example, the default option in ScanDisk for lost file clusters is to restore them as files. However, in almost every case, the restored files are unusable. You can change the default so ScanDisk simply throws these files away.

Suppose you've been working on your computer at the home office, and you are in the process of making changes to your customer address list. There are several entries that you've changed, and you're using the Save command to store the changes to the hard disk. Suddenly the lights flicker, go dim for a few brief moments, and then go out. After about 15 seconds, the power is restored, and your computer restarts. However, when you re-open the customer address file, you note that the changes weren't saved. You can make the changes again to the file, but you're puzzled: what happened to the changes? It's likely that they were written to a temporary file that wasn't completely closed, so a lost cluster has been created. In the next exercises, you start ScanDisk to locate any missing clusters and then configure it to throw away the lost clusters.

Start ScanDisk

1   Click Start, point to Programs, point to Accessories, point to System Tools, and then click ScanDisk.

The ScanDisk window appears.

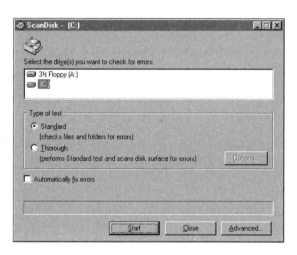

2   In the ScanDisk window, scroll through the Select The Drive(s) You Want To Check For Errors list, and select drive C.

3   Under Type Of Test, click Thorough.

The thorough test checks the disk for physical errors (bad sectors) as well as software errors (lost clusters).

4   Click the Automatically Fix Errors check box.

Selecting this option lets ScanDisk fix any errors it finds without requiring input from you.

5   Click the Advanced button.

The ScanDisk Advanced Options window appears.

6 Under Log File, select Append To Log.

This will keep a log file of all the ScanDisk actions.

7 Under Lost File Fragments, click Free.

This will find lost clusters, and free the disk space so it can be used again.

8 Click OK.

Run ScanDisk

In this exercise, you run ScanDisk using the changes you've made to the settings.

1 In the ScanDisk window, click the Start button.

When ScanDisk completes its work, the ScanDisk Results window appears.

2 Click the Close button, and then click the Close button again.

You don't have to use the Start menu to use ScanDisk, Backup, or Disk Defragmenter. You can start any of these disk tools from the drive's properties window. This can be a quick and efficient way to check a disk or back it up.

Run ScanDisk from a drive window

Suppose you're viewing the contents of a disk drive, and you ask yourself whether you've scanned the disk recently for disk errors. You can find out the last time you checked a drive for errors by opening the Properties dialog box for any drive. If you want, you can then start ScanDisk right from the Properties dialog box. In this exercise, you run ScanDisk on a floppy disk.

1 Insert the Practice Files disk into drive A.

2 Open My Computer and open drive A.

3 With the right mouse button, click a blank area in the drive A window.

4   Click Properties.

The Floppy (A:) Properties window appears.

5   Click the Tools tab.

6   Under Error-Checking Status, click Check Now.

ScanDisk opens.

7   Click Start, and then when the disk scan is complete, click Close.

8   Click Close again, and then click OK.

9   Click the Close button on the floppy drive window, and then click the Close button on the My Computer window.

Performing a Final Tune-up on Your Disk

The last thing you can do when you have run ScanDisk is to remove any CHK files from your root folder, and any TMP files from the C:\Windows\Temp folder. Whenever ScanDisk finds and fixes a lost file cluster, CHK files are created. Many programs create TMP files when files are being edited; if the program closes unexpectedly, such as when the power fails, TMP files might be left in the C:\Windows\Temp folder.

 IMPORTANT   The C:\Windows\Temp folder might contain copies of e-mail attachments or other files that you might find useful. Be careful that you do not simply erase all the files in the C:\Windows\Temp folder without examining its contents.

In the following exercises, you open the root folder of your hard disk, remove the CHK files, open the C:\Windows\Temp folder, and remove any TMP files.

Remove the CHK files

1   Double-click the My Computer icon, and then double-click drive C.

2   On the View menu of the drive C window, point to Arrange Icons, and then click Type.

The file icons are sorted by type.

If the ScanDisk option to free lost clusters is active, there should be no new CHK files in this folder.

3   Hold down CTRL and click any files in the drive C window that have the CHK file type.

4   Hold down SHIFT and press DELETE.

Holding down SHIFT as you press DELETE bypasses the Recycle Bin and immediately deletes the files from the disk.

5   Click Yes.

The selected files are erased.

Remove the TMP files

 ⚠ WARNING Before beginning this exercise, make sure that you are not running any other programs, such as Microsoft Word, that might need access to a temporary file. If at any time a message box appears informing you that you cannot delete a file because it is in use, just click OK. The file will probably be deleted automatically by whatever program is currently using it—if it is a temporary file.

1 Double-click the Windows folder, and then double-click the Temp folder.

2 Hold down CTRL and click any files that have the TMP extension.

3 Hold down SHIFT and press DELETE.

4 Hold down SHIFT and click the Close button on the Temp window.

Holding down SHIFT when you click the Close button closes the current window and any windows that were opened sequentially from the current window.

Running ScanDisk from a Shortcut

Suppose you've decided that you want to run ScanDisk frequently so that you can check the integrity of your hard disk. You can save time by creating a shortcut to ScanDisk and modifying its properties. The following options are available in ScanDisk. The options appear following the name of the ScanDisk program either in an MS-DOS window or as part of the program name in a shortcut.

Option	Result
/n	Scans the disk, but does not stop for user input.
/p	Scans the disk, but does not make changes or fix errors.
/a	Scans all local (non-networked), nonremoveable (fixed) disks.
drive:	Scans the drive specified.

Create and run a ScanDisk shortcut

In this exercise, you create a shortcut to run ScanDisk automatically, and then you use it.

If your Windows 95 folder is not on drive C or is not named "Windows," click Browse and then locate Scandskw.exe in your Windows 95 folder.

1 Use the right mouse button to click the Desktop, point to New, and then click Shortcut.

2 In the Command Line box, type **c:\windows\scandskw.exe** (the path to the ScanDisk program) and then click Next.

3 In the Select A Name For The Shortcut box, type **Scan Drive C** and then click Finish.

4 Use the right mouse button to click the shortcut Scan Drive C, and then click Properties.

5 Click the Shortcut tab, and place the insertion point at the end of the Target box.

6 Press the SPACEBAR, and then type **/n c:**

This sets ScanDisk to operate with no confirmation (/n) from you and to check drive C.

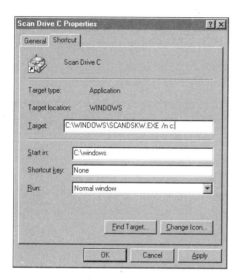

7 Click OK.

8 Double-click Scan Drive C.

ScanDisk starts checking drive C. When it's done, you're prompted to verify the results.

9 Click Close.

Optimizing Your Hard Disk

Each cluster on a hard disk can store a fixed number of bytes. When your hard disk stores a file, it puts pieces of the file into whatever cluster is free. This means that many files are stored in pieces that are separated from each other, and the operating system keeps track of where each file piece is located. This does not cause problems when retrieving a file, because each file piece is assembled automatically when it is retrieved and the pieces are returned to their proper sequence. However, your hard disk performs most efficiently when files are stored in a contiguous stream, because the disk's read/write heads do not need to wait for the disk to spin around several times in order to find all the pieces.

You can optimize the use of your hard disk by *defragmenting* it. Defragmenting the hard disk puts the pieces of each file into one contiguous file stream.

Suppose you've been using your home office computer for several months, running a program to keep track of your customer list. Your assistant, Pat Lee, spends about 15 hours a week making changes, updating invoices, adding customer addresses, processing orders, and sending and receiving faxes. Although you are careful to delete unwanted files as soon as you can, you notice that each week there's slightly less space to work with. Also, loading the customer list takes slightly longer each week. You've decided that the main reason for the problem is that the files on the hard disk have become fragmented.

Optimize your disk with Disk Defragmenter

In this exercise, you use Disk Defragmenter to group your files into contiguous clusters.

 NOTE Defragmenting your hard disk can take a long time, especially if you have a large hard disk. Plan on spending about 20 minutes to several hours waiting for the defragmentation process to be completed.

1 Click Start, point to Programs, point to Accessories, point to System Tools, and then click Disk Defragmenter.

2 In the Which Drive Do You Want To Defragment? window, select drive C.

3 Click OK.

The Disk Defragmenter window appears.

4 Click Start.

5 Click the Show Details button.

The Defragmenting Drive C window expands to show a graphic representation of the defragmentation process.

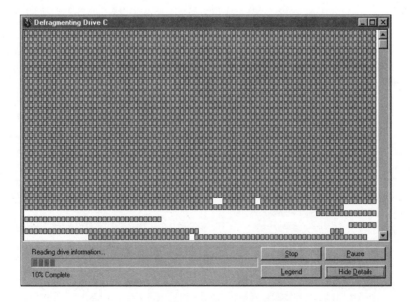

6   Click the Legend button.

The legend explains what the different colors in the defragmentation screen mean.

7   Click the Close button.

The defragmentation process continues.

8   When the defragmentation is finished, click OK.

Compressing Your Hard Disk

Disk compression reduces the amount of space required to store file information, which increases the total storage capacity of a disk. You can use DriveSpace, an optional component of Windows 95, to compress the data on your disk and increase the amount of available space. Often you can double the total disk capacity of your hard disk. DriveSpace gives you more space by creating a *compressed volume file* or CVF that appears to your programs as if it were a new hard disk with approximately twice the capacity of the original hard disk.

For example, if you have a 250-MB hard disk with 150 MB free space, after compression of the entire disk you would effectively have a "new" 500-MB hard disk with approximately 400 MB free space. The 100 MB of used space would still appear as 100 MB, but the 250 MB hard drive is now able to store 500 MB. The same 100 MB of data is now only occupying 20% of the available disk space, instead of the 40% it occupied before the disk was compressed. The physical hard drive, called the *host drive*, is assigned a new drive letter, such as K, and is hidden from view in My Computer.

There are two basic options for compressing a hard disk. Each has its advantages and disadvantages. The following table compares the two options.

Compression option	Advantages	Disadvantages
Entire disk	Creates most space.	Takes the longest time to create the compressed disk.
Free space only	Quickest method to create a new disk.	Does not make maximum use of the original hard disk.

NOTE   If you compress the hard disk that contains Windows 95, DriveSpace will restart the computer during the compression process and load a limited version of Windows 95. Do not stop DriveSpace at this point in the process. After the compression procedure is complete, your computer will restart Windows 95.

Using the DriveSpace Program

Suppose you've been working on your home office computer for several months, creating, saving, deleting, and changing files. When you first purchased the computer, you were confident that you had enough disk space to hold all your data. Now you're finding that you're running out of room. You aren't ready yet to buy a larger hard disk. To resolve this lack of disk space, you decide to use DriveSpace to compress part of your disk and gain more room.

 NOTE   You should back up your hard disk before you use DriveSpace to compress it.

Install DriveSpace

In this exercise, you install the DriveSpace component.

1   Click the Start menu, point to Settings, and then click Control Panel.

2   In the Control Panel window, double-click the Add/Remove Programs icon.

3   In the Add/Remove Programs Properties dialog box, click the Windows Setup tab.

4   In the Windows Setup tab window, click the Disk Tools option.

5   Click the Details button.

If DriveSpace is not visible in this list, it's already installed. Click Cancel, and skip to the next exercise.

6   In the Disk Tools dialog box, scroll downward and click DriveSpace.

7   Click OK, and then click OK again.

Windows Setup begins installing the DriveSpace component. You might be asked to insert a disk or CD. Click OK to complete the process.

8   On the Control Panel window, click the Close button.

 NOTE   If you are currently using another compression program, you will not be able to use DriveSpace at the same time.

Compress your hard disk

In this exercise, you start and configure DriveSpace, creating a new compressed drive H from 2 MB of existing space on drive C.

1   Click Start, point to Programs, point to Accessories, point to System Tools, and then click DriveSpace.

The DriveSpace window appears.

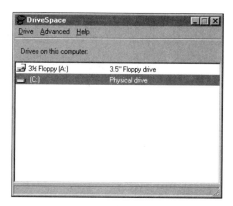

To compress your entire drive C, skip steps 3 and 4, and click Compress on the Drive menu. Compressing an entire hard disk can take a considerable amount of time. It is therefore not recommended for this exercise.

2 In the Drives On This Computer List, select drive C.

3 On the Advanced menu, click Create Empty.

The Create New Compressed Drive dialog box appears.

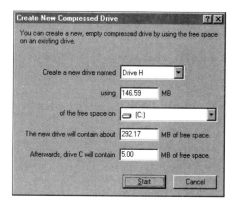

4 Double-click in the Using text box, and then type **2**

DriveSpace will create a new compressed drive out of 2 MB of unused space from your drive C. The New Drive Will Contain About text box is probably showing 3 MB. This number is estimated by using the compression ratio of approximately 1.6 to 1.

5 In the Drive Letter Of Host Drive box, select H.

6 Click Start.

DriveSpace first scans your drive C for any possible errors or defects. If it locates any, a dialog box will appear instructing you to run ScanDisk before you can successfully create a new compressed drive. If DriveSpace doesn't find any errors, it will create the new drive and return to the Create New Compressed Drive dialog box. At this time, you could create additional new compressed drives.

7   Click Close.

The Restart Computer dialog box appears. To access your newly created drive, you need to restart your computer.

Remove any disks that might be in your A or B drive before clicking Yes.

8   Click Yes.

The Restart dialog box appears. After a moment or two your computer restarts.

 TROUBLESHOOTING   If you receive an error message each time you run DriveSpace that instructs you to run ScanDisk, but you have run ScanDisk before, there might be disk errors that ScanDisk is not able to fix automatically. Start ScanDisk and make sure the Automatically Fix Errors check box is not checked. Usually, as you run ScanDisk, you'll be able to determine how to correct any errors from the information given in ScanDisk. However, if the condition persists, you should contact a qualified service professional.

Check the new compressed drive

Now that you have created a new drive, you'll want to make sure that everything has turned out as you expected.

1   Double-click the My Computer icon.

The My Computer window appears showing the available drives on your computer.

2   Using the right mouse button, click the compressed drive H, and then click Properties on the shortcut menu.

The Properties window for the compressed volume appears and shows the amount of available space. This should be roughly equal to what was displayed in the Create New Compressed Drive dialog box.

Removing a Compressed Drive

Although it's not a common action, you can remove a compressed drive and replace it with its original format and size. The process of removing a large compressed drive can take a long time, as DriveSpace must decompress the data on the drive, free up some space on the host drive, and then move the data to the host drive. This process must be done over and over again until all the data is moved back to the host drive. If you have filled the compressed drive with data, you cannot uncompress it successfully until you remove enough data to allow it to fit on the original host drive.

Uncompress the compressed drive

You've decided that you want to uncompress the compressed drive. You'll use DriveSpace to move the data from the CVF to the host drive, and then remove the compressed drive.

1   Click Start, point to Programs, point to Accessories, point to System Tools, and then click DriveSpace.

2 Click drive H.

3 On the Drive menu, click Uncompress.

The Uncompress A Drive window appears during the process.

4 Click Close.

The drive is uncompressed.

5 Click Yes to restart Windows 95.

One Step Further: Changing the Assumed Compression Ratio

The amount of free space listed as available on a compressed drive is just an estimate based on how much data could potentially be stored there. The compression software makes an estimate about how much files are compressed. This estimate is based on the compression ratio. For example, the compression ratio of 2 to 1 means that for every byte of actual disk space, you can probably get two bytes stored in your CVF.

Certain types of files can be highly compressed and others can't. Files containing a lot of text can usually be highly compressed. Programs and most multimedia files cannot be compressed very much. (Typically, multimedia files have already been compressed.) When you copy a file to your compressed disk, it will be compressed as much as possible, which might be 3 to 1. However, the compression software will still estimate your free disk space based on the compression ratio used to compress the disk, which in this case would be 2 to 1.

Suppose you're running low on free disk space, but you've already used DriveSpace to create a compressed drive. Most of your files contain text only, so you think that these files are actually compressed at a higher ratio than the default ratio of 2 to 1. By changing the assumed compression ratio, you will be able to increase the amount of available disk space for storing additional files. To do this, you'll use DriveSpace to change the assumed compression ratio for your drive.

In the following exercises, you'll first create a new compressed drive similar to the one you created and then deleted earlier in this lesson. You'll copy a few files to the new drive to determine the actual compression ratio. Then, you'll change the drive's compression ratio based on the actual amount of data compression on your new drive.

NOTE The compression ratio results in this One Step Further exercise are based on a 200 MB hard disk configured as a single drive (partition). Because the total capacity of a disk will affect the actual compression ratio, the numbers you see on your screen will probably differ from those you see in this book.

Create the new compressed drive

Because you created a compressed drive earlier in this lesson, the following steps are condensed. If you need more detailed instruction, refer to the previous exercise "Compress your hard disk."

1   Start DriveSpace, click drive C, and then click Create Empty on the Advanced menu.

The Create New Compressed Drive dialog box appears.

2   Double-click in the Using text box , type **2**, and then select drive H for the new drive letter.

3   Click Start. After the new drive is created, click Close, and then click Yes to restart your computer.

Copy files to the new drive and determine the actual compression ratio

To see how much compression your new drive can achieve with your data, you'll copy a few files to your new drive.

TROUBLESHOOTING   You might not actually have enough disk space on a compressed disk to install a new program, even though the operating system is reporting sufficient space. Program files do not compress very well, and because of this they might require more disk space than is actually available. If you receive an error during the installation of a program to a compressed disk, try installing the program to another, non-compressed disk, or freeing up more space on your compressed disk.

---

1   Double-click the My Computer Icon, and then double-click the icon for drive C.

The window displaying the files and folders on drive C appears.

2   Double-click the More Windows SBS Practice folder icon.

The More Windows SBS Practice window displays the files and folders it contains.

You'll probably have to drag the windows apart so you can see them at the same time.

3   Double-click the Storage folder in the More Windows SBS Practice folder window, and then drag the Mostly Empty text file and the My Report Word file to the icon for drive H in the My Computer window.

Both files are copied to drive H.

4   On the taskbar, click the My Computer button to display its window. Then use the right mouse button to click the icon for drive H, and click properties on the short-cut menu. Make sure the General tab is active.

The (H:) Properties window appears.

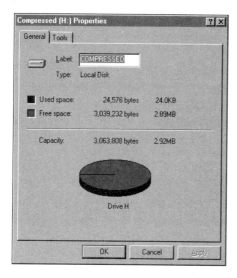

5 Click the Close button in the upper-right corner of the Properties window.

Change the compression ratio for the new drive

Now that the new compressed drive has a few files on it, you want to know what kind of compression you are actually achieving. You'll use this information to modify the compression ratio for this drive.

1 Start DriveSpace, click drive H, and then click Properties on the Drive menu.

The Compression Properties Drive H dialog box appears. It looks similar to the following illustration.

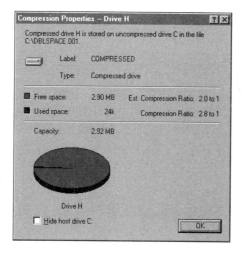

2 Use the right mouse button to click the label text Est. Compression Ratio, and then click What's This?

A Tip Window appears explaining the estimated compression ratio.

3 Repeat step 2 for the label text Compression Ratio.

A Tip Window appears explaining the actual compression ratio.

4 Click the Close button on the dialog box, and then click Change Ratio on the Advanced menu in the DriveSpace dialog box.

The Compression Ratio For Compressed (H) dialog box appears.

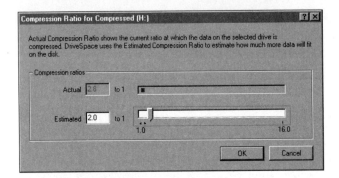

5 Double-click in the Estimated text box, and then type **2.5**

Even though the actual compression ratio for this drive H is 2.8 to 1 you will probably not be able to consistently achieve that high of a compression ratio. To avoid the potential problem of running out of actual disk space later on, you'll use a compression ratio of 2.5 to 1 and plan to monitor the actual compression ratio periodically.

6 Click OK, read the information in the Drive In Use dialog box, and then click Yes.

The Restart Dialog box appears. Windows 95 then restarts in a special mode to make the changes to your compressed drive H. When Windows 95 has completed this operation, the DriveSpace Operation Complete dialog box appears.

7 Click OK.

Windows 95 restarts in its normal mode.

Check the new capacity for drive H and then delete it

Now that the new compressed drive has had the compression ratio changed, you'll want to check the amount of free space reported by the operating system. Then you'll decide that the new size is insufficient, so you'll delete the compressed drive.

1 Start DriveSpace, select drive H, and then click Properties on the Drive menu.

The Compression Properties dialog box appears. The dialog box field Capacity is probably showing 3.65 MB. Because you are using such a small (2 MB) amount of actual storage space, the effective compression ratio is less than what you would expect. You decide that even at a compression ratio of 2.5 to 1 the drive is too small to be really useful, so you'll delete it.

2 Click the Close button in the upper-right corner of the Compression Properties dialog box, and then click Delete on the Advanced menu.

 ⚡**WARNING**   Any data on the compressed drive will be lost permanently if you click Yes. Make sure there are only the copied practice files (Mostly Empty and My Report) on drive H before continuing with this exercise.

If you see the Remove Compression? dialog box, click Yes to free up the memory used by the driver.

3 In the dialog box, click Yes.

The compressed drive is deleted along with all the data stored on the drive. The DriveSpace Operation Complete dialog box appears.

4 Click OK.

The Restart Computer dialog box appears.

5 Click Yes.

Windows restarts.

If you want to continue to the next lesson

1 Remove the Practice Files disk from drive A or B.

2 Close all open windows.

If you want to quit Windows 95 for now

1 Remove the Practice Files disk from drive A or B.

2 Close all open windows.

3 On the Start menu, click Shut Down.

4 Click Shut Down The Computer? and then click Yes.

Lesson Summary

To	Do this
Back up data from your hard disk	Insert a tape into the tape device. Start Backup. Click OK, and then click OK again. Select the folders and files you want to back up. Click Next Step. Select the tape device icon. Click Start Backup. Type a name for the backup set. Click OK, and then click OK again. Close Backup.
Restore data to your hard disk	Insert the backup tape into the tape device. Start Backup. Click OK, and then click OK again. Click the Restore button. Select the tape device icon. Click Next Step. Select the files and folders to restore. Click Start Restore. Click OK, and then click OK again. Close Backup.
Find and fix common disk problems	Start ScanDisk. Select the drive to check. Click Start. Click Close, and then click Close again.
Defragment your hard disk	Start Disk Defragmenter. Select the drive to defragment. Click OK. Click Start. Click OK.
Create a compressed drive, using free space on your disk	Start DriveSpace. On the Advanced menu, click Create Empty. Enter the amount of free space to use and, optionally, the host drive letter. Click Start. Click Close.

To	Do this
Compress your entire hard disk	Start DriveSpace. Select the drive to compress. On the Drive menu, click Compress. Click Start. Click Compress Now. Click Close.
Decompress your hard disk	Start DriveSpace. Select the compressed drive to decompress. On the Drive menu, click Uncompress. Click Close.

For online information about	From the Help dialog box, click Index and then type
Backing up data from your hard disk	**backup**
Restoring data to your hard disk	**restoring**
Finding and fixing common disk problems	**ScanDisk**
Defragmenting your hard disk	**Disk Defragmenter**
Compressing your hard disk	**DriveSpace**

Preview of the Next Lesson

In Lesson 4, "Working with Network Resources," you'll learn how to work with a network server and connect to its resources. You'll also learn how to share your computer's resources, such as printers and file folders, with your your co-workers.

Working with Network Resources

Estimated time
40 min.

In this lesson you will learn how to:

■ Work with a network server.

■ Share resources on a network.

■ Modify access control rights.

■ Find network resources.

■ Connect your computer to network resources.

Most people in an office work in partnership with others, sharing file cabinets, bookshelves, and floor space. Often a resource, such as a printer, is centrally located so everyone can use it. Or, a resource might be in one person's office, yet all the team members must have access to it.

Sharing office resources maximizes use and minimizes cost. However, there can be problems in sharing resources. Sometimes you might not want everyone to have access to a resource, or you might want to restrict some people from certain resources, such as personnel records or payroll information. If that's the case, you must lock the cabinet and give the keys to only a few people.

You also might want to use a resource but you might not know who has it. For example, you might have a printer that's on a moveable cart. One day, you might have it in your work area; on another day, someone in the office down the hall might have it. Before you can use the printer, you must find out where it is, wheel it back down to your work area, and then connect it to your computer.

In this lesson, you learn how to work with resources that are in other locations. You learn how to find network resources, such as printers or folders, and how to map them to your own computer. You also learn how to set up access control levels to your resources, and how to share your resources with others on your network.

Working with a Network Server

In many workplaces, all the computers are connected on a *network* so that they can share information and resources. A network is composed of *workstations* (the individual computers) and cabling, network interface cards and network operating system software. In a *peer-to-peer* network, all the workstations have equal access to each other (they are *peers*), all can share resources, and all share the workload of transferring information across the network cabling. There is no central *server,* or single computer controlling distribution of information and resources. In a sense, every workstation on a peer-to-peer network could be considered a server to the other workstations.

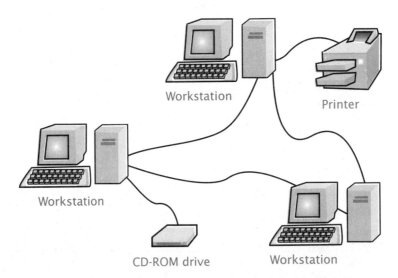

In a peer-to-peer network, all workstations and resources can be shared equally. Each workstation can function as both a server and a client.

For example, one workstation might have a printer connected to it, and another workstation might have a CD-ROM drive connected to it. Everyone on the network who has been authorized can access all the resources if the workstations with the peripheral hardware are turned on and running Windows 95, if peer resource sharing is enabled, and if the peripheral hardware is designated for sharing. However, if the workstation with the printer is turned off, no one can use the printer.

In a *client-server* network, all the shared resources are typically located on a separate computer, called the *network server*. The network server is a central computer that has the hardware and software to run the network services. The network server performs most of the work in this type of network.

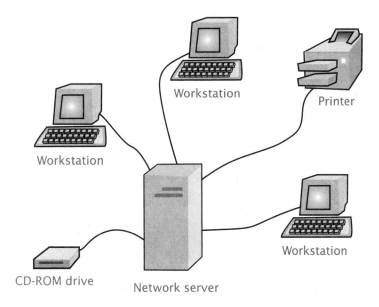

In a client-server network, all workstations (clients) and shared resources are connected to a central computer (network server). All shared data resides on the server.

A network server might be connected to printers, modems, shared applications (such as an electronic mail post office), or fax machines. If the workstations on a network are the muscles and the cabling that connects the computers are the nerves and spinal cord of the system, then the network server is the brain of a client-server network.

A client-server network helps to keep resource use at maximum efficiency. Often the network server is the fastest machine with the most memory and storage space. Also, in a client-server network, it's common to find that all of the resources (such as file storage devices, printers, fax modems, and CD-ROM drives) are connected to the network server in some way. You get access to a resource by connecting to the network server and then connecting to the resource.

A peer-to-peer network is often the easiest to set up and administer. You don't need to dedicate one computer just to operate the network. In a typical home or small office, a peer-to-peer network is often the best solution for connecting workstations to each other.

Not only do these two types of networks have their individual advantages, but they can be used in concert with one another. It is very likely that in a large corporate environment you will find a combination of peer-to-peer and client-server networking combined and operating together.

In the following discussions and exercises, a client-server network server or a shared-resource peer server will be referred to simply as a network server, unless the discussion or exercise applies to only one type of server.

Sharing Your Resources on the Network

You can share your resources on your network by setting up *access control rights*. Access control determines what rights you give to individuals or groups who are logged on to the network and want access to your files and resources. For example, you might have a folder that everyone in your workgroup can use, but another folder that you want only your assistant to use. You might have a folder that contains information that most people can view, but you want only your order entry clerk to update. You can protect the information in shared folders by using access control rights.

Sharing your resources involves three basic steps:

- Enable file and printer sharing
- Enable access control of your resources
- Share your resources

You enable file and printer sharing in the Network window. Then you can assign access control rights. After you assign access control rights, you can share your resources with other users and be confident that only approved users will gain access to sensitive data.

Enabling File and Printer Sharing

Windows 95 allows two types of file and printer sharing. Which one you use depends on the type of network to which your computer is connected, as well as the *network client* you've installed. The network client is the software connection between your workstation and the network. Windows 95 provides network clients for two popular networks, Client for Microsoft Networks and Client for NetWare Networks.

Windows 95 also supports other networks, but it does not supply network clients for them. You must contact the network vendor to get the network client that works with Windows 95 for other networks. Refer to the *Microsoft Windows 95 Resource Kit* (available from Microsoft Press and all good bookstores) for a list of networks that are supported by Windows 95.

Install file and printer sharing

Suppose you've set up your home office to use The Microsoft Network client. You want to enable file and printer sharing so that your assistant, Pat Lee, can gain access to your local hard disk and use the laser printer attached to your computer. In this exercise, you enable file and printer sharing.

1 Click Start. Point to Settings, and then click Control Panel.

2 Double-click Network, and then click the Configuration tab.

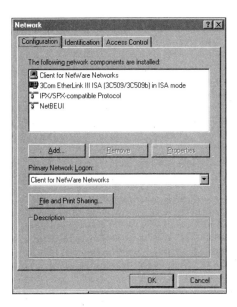

3 If File And Printer Sharing For Microsoft Networks does not appear in the list, click Add, click Service, click Microsoft, click File And Printer Sharing For Microsoft Networks, and then click OK.

You might be prompted to insert a Windows 95 Installation disk or the Windows 95 Upgrade CD. Insert the disk or CD, and click OK.

NOTE If you are using File and Printer sharing for NetWare Networks, you will see an error message. Click OK in the message box. Click the service in the list box, click Remove, and then repeat step 3.

---

4 Click OK, and then click Yes to restart your computer.

When you change your network configuration, you must restart your computer to use the new configuration.

5 Log onto Windows 95. Open Networks in Control Panel.

6 Click the File And Print Sharing button, and verify that both options are selected. If an option is not selected, select it and restart your computer. Click OK and then click OK again.

Setting Access Control Rights

After you enable file and printer sharing, you can grant other users access to your local resources by using *access control rights*. The access control rights determine who has access to the resources, and to what level each user has access to the resources.

There are two types of access control rights. The first, *share-level access control*, grants access to all users who know the correct password. Share level access control is a simple form of security that provides you with a means to control who can use a shared resource on your computer. With share level access control, you establish a password for each resource you share. When a person attempts to attach their computer to the shared resource, the password for that resource must be entered by the person. In addition, you can also have more than one password for a single shared resource if you want to allow access, but restrict what a person can do with the files and folders on that resource. For some resources, such as a shared CD-ROM drive, there would be no reason to establish different passwords.

Until you tell other people the password for your shared resource, no one can access the resource you are sharing. Every time you change the password, you must tell other people the new password for your shared resource. Also, any person who knows the password can access your shared resource, whether or not you intended the person to access your shared resource.

You can specify full access, read-only access, or both. It's a good idea to set separate passwords for full access and read-only access; otherwise, anyone can access the resources on your computer.

The second type of access control rights is *user-level access control*. Under user-level access control, you identify which users you want to have access to your resources, and then you can grant each user different access rights. You identify the users from a user list that resides on the network server and is maintained by a network administrator—a person in charge of handling technical and administrative tasks related to the use and operation of a network server. Because a user must be on the user list to have access to the network, the security in user-level access control is far greater than in share-level access control. Your computer must be connected to a supported server, such as a Windows NT server or a Novell NetWare server, to use user-level access control.

In either of the two access control methods, you can establish shared resources in almost any fashion you desire. For example, you can establish a separate shared resource for any folder on your hard disk, your entire hard disk, a CD-ROM drive in your computer, or a printer attached to your computer. These resources can be shared and available at the same time. You can also stop and start sharing any resources whenever you like. If you stop sharing a printer, for example, you do not have to stop sharing the folders on your hard disk.

SHARE-LEVEL ACCESS

USER-LEVEL ACCESS

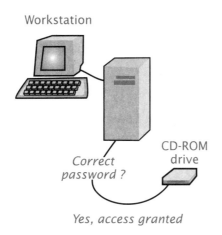

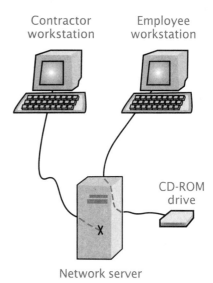

Access to the CD-ROM drive is gained by the user entering a password.

Access to the CD-ROM drive is granted to selected users through the network server.

Modifying Share-Level Access Control

Suppose you're working in your home office, where you've set up a small network. You want to set up file and printer sharing for your co-workers so that both Pat Lee and K.C. Brown can access your printers and files. You've already set up file and printer access. The next step is to set up share-level access.

First, you need to modify the access control rights to give users access to the resources connected to your computer. After you've installed the file and printer sharing services for Microsoft Networks, you can grant share-level access to users.

You can specify three types of share-level access: read-only, full, and none. Read-only access allows users who know the password to only view the contents of the files on your computer. Full access allows users who know the password to view, create, edit, save, and delete files. Although you do not need to establish passwords for share-level access, it's a good idea to use them to control who has access to the shared resources on your computer. If you do not use passwords with share-level access, anyone who can access your network can access your computer's shared resources.

NOTE You can only perform the following exercises if your computer is connected to a Microsoft-compatible network and is running a Windows 95 compatible client or Client For Microsoft Network. Otherwise, skip to the next section, "Modifying User-Level Access Control."

Set up share-level access

In this exercise, you'll select share-level access for your computer.

1 In the Control Panel window, double-click Networks.

2 Click the Access Control tab.

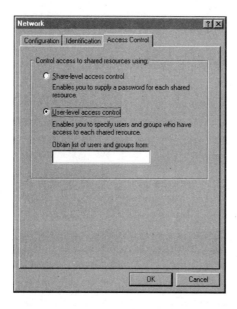

3 Click Share-Level Access Control.

4 Click OK.

Because you must restart Windows 95 when you add or change access control options, you might be prompted to shut down and restart Windows 95. Click Yes, and then log back on to Windows 95.

5 On the Control Panel window, click the Close button.

You can now grant access to your computer's resources to anyone on your network. However, you do not want K.C. Brown to be able to access some of the files that Pat Lee is working with. Also, most of the information on your computer you want to be kept private. You can assign different levels of security by establishing different passwords for various individuals.

You've decided to grant full access to your Storage folder so that anyone who knows the full access password can view, edit, save, and delete the information. You also want to grant read-only access to your storage folder so that anyone who knows the read-only password can see and view the files but not change them. You will set up two passwords, one for full access, and one for read-only access. Everyone else, who does not know either password cannot access any of your files.

Grant access rights to your Storage folder

In this exercise, you set up passwords to grant full access and read-only access to your Storage folder.

1   Open the More Windows SBS Practice folder in My Computer. Then, using the right mouse button, click the Storage folder.

2   Click Sharing, and then click the Sharing tab.

3   Click Shared As.

4   In the Share Name box, type **Presentation**

5   In the Comment box, type **This folder contains my presentation**

6   Click Depends On Password.

When you use share-level access, anyone who knows the correct password can access the shared resource.

7   In the Read-Only Password box, type **viewonly**

8   In the Full box, type **editall** and then click OK.

A window appears for you to verify the passwords.

9   In the Read-Only Password box, type **viewonly**

10   In the Full box, type **editall** and click OK.

Shared Resource

The folder is shared. Its icon (shown at left) is changed to show a hand holding the folder.

Now you can tell Pat that he can access your Storage folder from Network Neighborhood using the password "editall," and you can tell K.C. Brown that she can access your folder using the password "viewonly."

Modifying User-Level Access Control

If your computer is connected to a server, such as a Microsoft Windows NT server or a Novell NetWare server, you can use user-level access control to allow users pre-determined access to the resources connected to your computer. You can use user-level access control with most networks supported by Windows 95. You *cannot* use user-level access controls in a peer-to-peer only network because there is no appropriate type of server to validate the users.

If your computer is connected to a Microsoft Windows NT server or a Novell NetWare server, you can grant nine areas of access control rights to users. These access control rights are for disk drives and folders. The following table lists the access control rights you can grant.

Access control	Abbreviation	Permitted activities
List Files	F	View the list of files in a folder
Read Files	R	Read the contents of files
Write Files	W	Open and change existing files. Cannot create new files
Create Files and Folders	C	Create new files and folders
Delete Files	D	Delete existing files
Change File Attributes	T	Change the attributes of files
Change Access Control	A	Change access control of files
Full Access Rights	U	Perform all operations on files
Read-Only Access Rights	O	View the list of files and read the contents of files. (Same as F and R)

Each access control right is self-contained; that is, granting the right to delete files does not give the user the right to read or write files.

Granting a user full access rights means that the user can perform every operation in the folder as if you were doing it. Granting read-only access rights is the same as granting list files access and read files access.

Let's say that you're back at your corporate office and you're going to connect to the corporate network, which uses a Windows NT server to run the network. You want to allow others connected to the network to access certain files on your computer using user-level access controls. First you'll set up user-level access control for these files. Then you'll give full access rights to your office assistant, Pat Lee. You'll grant read-only access to your office co-worker, K.C. Brown.

NOTE   To perform the following exercises on user-level access, your computer must be connected to a network that has a Novell NetWare server or a Windows NT server. If not, you can skip to the next section, "Finding Network Resources." If you are connected to a Novell NetWare network, you must specify the File And Printer Sharing For NetWare Networks service in the Network dialog box on the Configuration tab. See the exercise "Install File and Printer Sharing," earlier in this lesson, for information on how to select a different network service.

Set up user-level access control

In this exercise, you enable user-level access control for the resources on your computer.

You can also click Start, point to Settings, and then click Control Panel.

1 Double-click My Computer, and then click Control Panel.

2 Double-click the Network icon.

3 Click the Access Control tab, and then click User-Level Access Control if it's not selected.

   The settings for the Access Control appear.

4 Under Obtain List Of Users And Groups From, type the name of the server you usually log on to, or the name of the server that contains the user IDs of the people to whom you want to grant access.

   Typically, you type the name of a Windows NT server or a Novell NetWare server.

5 Click OK.

   The Network window closes. The System Settings Change window appears.

6 Click Yes.

   Windows 95 restarts. Log on to Windows 95 using your name and password.

Assign access control rights to users

Setting user-level access control levels is the same whether you use the Client For Microsoft Networks or the Client For NetWare Networks.

Now that you've set up user-level access control, you can specify what access Pat Lee, your assistant, and K.C. Brown, your office worker, have to your Storage folder.

In this exercise, you grant Pat Lee full access and K.C. Brown read-only access to the Storage folder. You also grant everyone in the Marketing group access to read and write the files.

1 In the More Windows SBS Practice folder, use the right mouse button to click the Storage folder, and then click Sharing.

   The Storage Properties window appears.

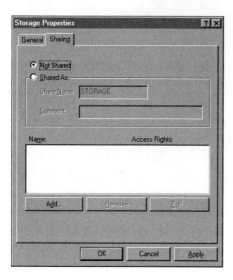

2 On the Sharing tab, click Shared As.

3 In the Share Name box, type **Presentation**

4 In the Comments box, type **This is my presentation**

5 Click the Add button.

The Add Users window appears.

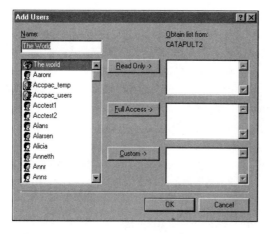

6 Click the entry for Pat Lee (or any individual name), and then click Full Access.

7 Click K.C. Brown (or any individual name), and then click Read Only.

8 Click Marketing (or any group), and then click Custom.

9 Click OK.

Because you selected Custom for the Marketing group, the Change Access Rights window appears for the Marketing group.

10 Under Custom Access Rights, click the options for [R]ead Files and [W]rite To Files, and then click OK.

The Marketing group will be allowed to read and change existing files; however, the users in that group will not be allowed to create new files or delete existing files. The Storage Properties window displays the settings for the three types of users.

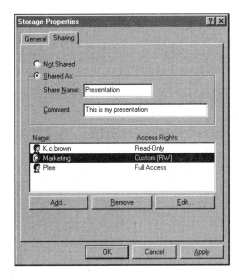

11 Click OK.

12 Hold down the SHIFT key and, on the More Windows SBS Practice window, click the Close button. Close any other open windows on the Desktop.

Holding down the SHIFT key while clicking the Close button on the current window will also close all of the windows you had to open to get to the current window.

Finding Network Resources

Suppose you need to open a summary presentation file created by Pat Lee, your assistant in your home office. He's created the file on his computer and left you a message telling you that the file is complete. You know it's on his computer, but you don't remember the name of his computer. Before you can open the file, you must locate the folder on the server where it's stored. You use Network Neighborhood to locate the server and then open the folder.

Before you can use a network resource, you must locate it. You can use Network Neighborhood to locate network resources attached to network servers. For example, if a laser printer is connected to the network server, you must open Network Neighborhood and then open the server to locate the laser printer.

NOTE This exercise assumes that both you and Pat Lee are connected to a network, and that Pat Lee has authorized others to access his files and printers. Pat Lee's computer's name is Plee. To complete this exercise, you can use any other computer name and folder name you want. If you do not have access to a network, you cannot complete this exercise.

Locate network resources

In this exercise, you use Network Neighborhood to find network resources. Although this exercise assumes that you have a peer-to-peer network set up in your home office, you can use the same techniques to find a network resource on a client-server network.

Network Neighborhood

1   Double-click the Network Neighborhood icon.

The Network Neighborhood window appears. The Network Neighborhood window shows only the network and servers that were attached during the startup of Windows 95.

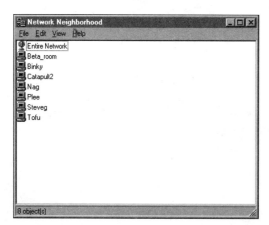

If you are not connected to a running network, you will receive an error message when you try to open the Entire Network window.

2   Double-click Entire Network.

Depending on the size of your network, it might take a few moments before the Entire Neighborhood window displays all the available network servers and workgroups. Note that your system administrator can modify your network settings so that some network resources might not appear in this window.

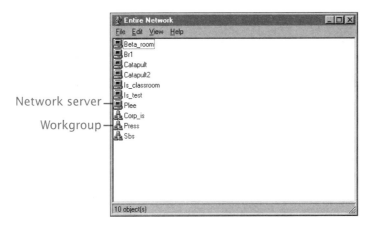

Network server —

Workgroup —

3 Open Plee (or whatever server is available).

The Plee window appears.

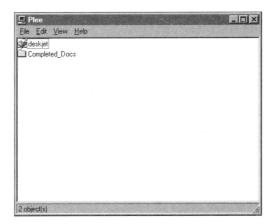

4 In the Plee window, open the Completed_Docs folder (or whatever folder is available).

5 Locate a file in the Completed_Docs folder, and drag it to your Desktop.

The file is copied to your Desktop from the Completed_Docs folder.

6 Close the Completed_Docs window.

Creating Shortcuts to Network Resources

After you've found a network resource such as a folder, you can *map* it as a local drive using Network Neighborhood. Mapping a network resource connects it to your computer as a local resource, and helps you find the resource easily. If the resource is a disk or folder, the new mapped resource will appear in My Computer as a new disk drive. If the resource is a printer, the new mapped resource will appear in the Printer folder in the Control Panel. Other devices, such as a fax/modem, might only appear in Network Neighborhood.

Map a network drive

Suppose you've located a network folder that contains files you use frequently. You can map that folder as a network drive. After you've mapped the folder to a drive letter, the drive icon appears in My Computer.

In this exercise, you map a network drive.

1 Click the Completed_Docs folder (or an available folder on a network drive).

2 On the File menu, click Map Network Drive.

The Map Network Drive window appears.

3 In the Drive box, click H (or whatever drive is available).

4 Click on the Reconnect At Logon box.

Specifying Reconnect At Logon ensures that the same drive will be mapped the same way the next time you start Windows 95.

5 Depending on the type of network your are using, you might need to click the Connect As Root Of The Drive box.

Selecting this option opens the drive as the first and topmost folder on Plee. This will hide from view all of the files and folders that are not inside the Completed_Docs folder.

6 Click OK.

The network drive is mapped to Drive H. The Completed_Docs On Plee (H:) window appears.

7 On the Completed_Docs On Plee (H:) window, click the Close button.

The window closes.

8 Click the Close button on all other open windows.

WARNING You can map more than one drive letter to the same network resource. For example, you could also map drive L (if it's not already in use) to the network folder Completed_Docs On Plee. You could then double-click the drive icons in My Computer for drive H and drive L and see exactly the same thing in both windows. Don't delete the contents of one window thinking you have a copy of the files in the other window.

Opening a Network Drive

When you first map a network drive, it is automatically opened for you. You can begin using the files in the folder, or you can close the folder and refer to its contents later.

After you've mapped a network drive, you use My Computer to open it. You can also open the folder directly from the Network Neighborhood.

Open a network drive

Suppose you have a set of files on Pat Lee's computer that you will need to access frequently. You know you can open his computer and get the files, so you decide to use the network drive. In this exercise, you open a network drive.

1   Double-click the My Computer icon.

The My Computer window opens. The network drive H icon appears in the window.

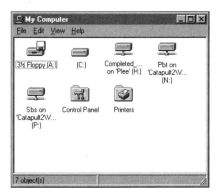

2   Double-click Drive H:

The Completed_Docs on Plee (H:) window opens.

83

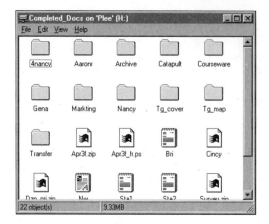

3   On the Completed_Docs on Plee (H:) window, click the Close button.

Removing a Network Drive

You might decide you no longer want to see a network drive. Perhaps the network is no longer available, or you do not have use for the files on it any longer. You can remove a network drive by disconnecting it.

NOTE   Removing a network drive does not delete its contents. It merely removes the icon from your Desktop. You can put the network drive back at any time.

Remove a network drive

Suppose you determine that you want to remove the network drive from My Computer. In this exercise, you remove a network drive. •

You can also use the right mouse button to click the network drive icon in the My Computer window and then click Disconnect on the shortcut menu.

1   Double-click the My Computer icon.

2   Click the Completed_Docs on Plee (H:) icon.

3   On the File menu, click Disconnect.

The drive is disconnected, and its icon is removed from the My Computer window. This also removes the Reconnect At Logon option for this network resource.

Attaching and Configuring a Remote Printer

Often a network server will have a printer connected to it. In this case, the network server is called a *print server* and its job is to manage the use of one or more printers. To use a printer on the network that is not physically connected to your computer, you must *attach* it. *Attaching* a network printer enables you to use the printer as if it were connected directly to your computer.

You can attach a network printer by using Network Neighborhood. After the printer is attached, you might need to install the printer driver for it. After you have installed the printer driver, you can configure the printer, to specify the paper orientation and size, and the paper bin to use.

Suppose there is an HP DeskJet 500 printer attached to Pat Lee's workstation. You decide to attach to his printer so that you can use it to print your documents.

Attach a remote printer

In this exercise you use the Add Printer wizard to attach your computer to Pat Lee's printer. If a printer driver needs to be installed, the wizard will prompt you for the Windows 95 disk or CD containing the driver.

1 Double-click the Network Neighborhood icon.

2 Double-click Plee (or any available server with a printer attached).

3 Click the HP DeskJet 500 (or any available printer).

You can also click Start, point to Settings, and then click Printers.

4 On the File menu, click Install.

The Add Printer Wizard window appears.

5 Under the text "Do You Print From MS-DOS–Based Programs?" click No if you do not print from MS-DOS–based programs. Click Yes if you print from MS-DOS–based programs, and then specify the printer port you want to use for the network printer.

Typically, Windows 95 can print directly to a network printer without having to associate a printer port, such as LPT1, to the network printer. However, MS-DOS–based programs still require use of a printer port. The Add Printer Wizard appears and lists printer manufacturers and printer models.

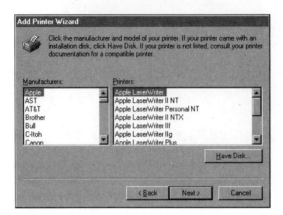

6 Under the Manufacturers list, click HP (or the printer manufacturer for the printer).

7 Under the Printers list, click the HP DeskJet 500 (or the printer model for the printer you are using), and then click Next.

The Add Printer Wizard window displays a proposed printer name.

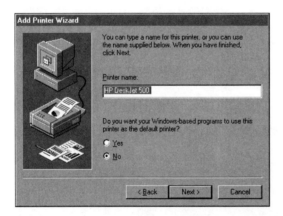

8 In the Printer Name box, type **My Printer**

9 Under Do You Want Your Windows-Based Programs To Use This Printer As The Default Printer, click Yes and click Next.

Click No if you do not want to use this printer as the default printer. The Add Printer Wizard window displays a prompt for you to test the printer settings.

10 Under "Would You Like To Print A Test Page?" click Yes, and then click Finish.

If you do not want to print a test page, click No.

11 If prompted, insert the requested Windows 95 disks or CD-ROM and then click OK.

After a few moments, the Printer Test Page Completed window appears.

12   Click Yes.

Select the printer configuration

When you install a printer, it is configured for its default settings. For example, most printers are set to print 1 copy of each document in portrait (tall) orientation. After you've connected to the network printer, you can change its configuration. For example, you might want to change from portrait or landscape (wide), or you might want to change the number of copies printed by default. You can change the properties of a network printer as easily as you can those of a locally attached printer.

In this exercise, you change some of the properties of the printer you installed. This will set the default options for the documents you print.

1   Double-click the My Computer icon, and then double-click Printers.

2   In the Printers window, click My Printer. On the File menu, click Properties.

The properties window for the printer appears.

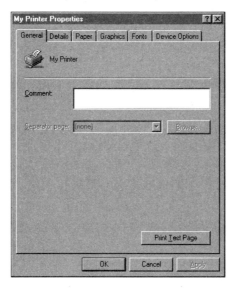

3 Click the General tab, and type **This is my network printer** in the Comment box.

4 Click the Paper tab, and then, under Orientation, click Landscape.

This resets the page orientation from portrait (tall) to landscape (wide).

5 Under Orientation, click Portrait.

The orientation is reset.

6 Click OK.

7 On the My Computer window, click the Close button.

 TIP   You can also modify the settings for any document and then save those specific settings as part of the document by using Microsoft Word, for example.

Printing to a Network Printer

You can easily print to a network printer (or any printer) by dragging a document to the printer icon in the Network Neighborhood window. When you are printing the document, a printer icon appears in the taskbar. You can double-click the printer icon in the taskbar to see a list of the print jobs waiting to be printed. Before a print job is actually printed, it is usually copied, or *spooled*, to a disk file on the server. *Spool* is an acronym for simultaneous print operations on line. By spooling files and using a print server, multiple print jobs are printed as soon as printer resources are available, allowing you to move on to other tasks. To view print jobs that are in progress or pending, you can open the print queue.

Create a printer shortcut

In this exercise, you create a shortcut to a network printer.

1 Drag the printer icon from the Printers window to your Desktop.

A dialog box prompts you to create a shortcut.

2 Click Yes.

The shortcut to the printer is created.

3 Use the right mouse button to click the new printer shortcut.

The shortcut menu appears.

4 Click Rename.

5 Type **My Printer** and press ENTER.

6 On the Printers window, click the Close button.

Print a document

In this exercise, you print a document by dropping it on the printer's shortcut icon.

1   Double-click the More Windows SBS Practice folder.

2   Drag the file My Report to the My Printer shortcut.

You might have to move the More Windows SBS Practice window to see the shortcut. The file begins printing. A printer icon appears in the taskbar.

3   Double-click the printer icon in the taskbar.

The My Printer window appears. The number of jobs in the print queue is displayed in the status bar of the window.

4   Click the Close button on the My Printer window and the More Windows SBS Practice window.

One Step Further: Creating a Shortcut to a Network Resource

After you've identified the network resources you need to use regularly, you can create shortcuts for them so you can use them without opening several folders. The default location for these new shortcuts is on the Desktop.

Create a shortcut to a network resource

Suppose, for example, that you have a network folder that you use often. You can access the folder in Network Neighborhood, but you decide you want to have a shortcut on the Desktop so that you can open it more easily. In this exercise, you create a shortcut for a folder.

1   Double-click Network Neighborhood.

2   Click Server1 (or any available server with a printer attached).

3   Click the Public folder (or any available folder).

4   On the File menu, click Create Shortcut.

Because you cannot create a shortcut in the Network Neighborhood folder, the Shortcut message window appears.

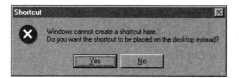

5 Click Yes.

The shortcut is created on the Desktop.

6 In the Public window, click the Close button.

7 In the Network Neighborhood window, click the Close button.

A shortcut to the public folder is saved on your Desktop.

If you want to continue to the next lesson

➤ Close all open windows.

If you want to quit Windows 95 for now

1 Close all open windows.

2 Click Start, and then click Shut Down.

3 Click Shut Down The Computer? and then click Yes.

Lesson Summary

To	Do this
Find a network resource	Open Network Neighborhood. Open Entire Network. Open the server that has the resource connected to it.
Map a network drive	Open Network Neighborhood. Open the server. Select the drive folder you want to map. On the File menu, click Map Network Drive. Select a drive letter to map the folder to, and click OK.
Open a network drive	Open My Computer. Open the mapped network drive.
Remove a network drive	Open My Computer. Select the network drive icon. On the File menu, click Disconnect.
Attach a remote printer	Open Network Neighborhood. Open the server. Select a printer icon. On the File menu, click Install. Follow the prompts in the Add Printer Wizard window.

To	Do this
Modify the Access Control for a folder	Open My Computer, and then open Control Panel. Open the Network icon. Click the Access Control tab. In the Obtain List of Users and Groups From box, type the name of the server that contains the information about authorized users. Click OK.
Assign user access controls	Open My Computer. Select the drive you want to share, or open a drive and select a folder you want to share. On the File menu, click Sharing. On the Sharing tab click Shared As. Type a share name in the Share Name box. Click the Add button. Select a user name in the left box, and then click Full Access, Read Only, or Custom. Click OK. If prompted, click the appropriate access levels, and then click OK.

For online information about	From the Help dialog box, click Index and then type
Mapping network drives	**mapping**
Mapping printers	**mapping**
Assigning access control rights	**access control**
Enabling user profiles	**user profiles**

Preview of the Next Lesson

In the next lesson, you'll work with The Microsoft Network. You'll learn to create and modify your user account. You'll view bulletin boards, chat with other Microsoft Network users, and send and receive files.

Review & Practice

In the lessons in Part 1, you learned skills to help you customize your computer, manage your hard disk, and work with network resources. If you want to practice these skills and test your understanding before you proceed with the lessons in Part 2, you can work through the Review & Practice section following this lesson.

Review & Practice

Estimated time
25 min.

- Back up and restore files.
- Find and fix common disk problems.
- Optimize and compress your hard disk.
- Customize your startup files.
- Work with a network server.
- Set up user profiles.

Before you go on to Part 2, you can practice the skills you learned in Part 1 by working through the steps in this Review & Practice section.

Scenario

You have successfully set up the computers in your home office. Because of the increase in your work load, your corporate office has loaned you another computer to add to your home office. You'll need to set up the computer, perform routine disk maintenance, install a new Plug and Play card, and set up network access.

Step 1: Set Up the Computer

In this step, you'll set up the additional computer to gain the most use from its hard drive. First you'll back up the files on the new computer. Then you'll use ScanDisk to check the hard disk for errors. You'll defragment the new hard disk and then compress the hard disk. Finally, you'll create a shortcut in the Startup folder so that each time Windows 95 is started the hard disk is checked for errors.

Install the Backup component

▶ Install the Backup component from Windows 95. (Hint: Start Add Remove Programs in Control Panel.)

Back up the files on your computer

1 Start Backup.
2 Back up the contents of the More Windows SBS Practice folder to a backup file on a tape drive or disk.
3 Quit Backup.

Find and fix common disk problems

1 With Windows 95 running, start ScanDisk.
2 Set the options to discard file fragments, and then run ScanDisk.
3 Close ScanDisk.

Optimize your hard disk

1 Start Disk Defragmenter.
2 Optimize drive C.

Compress your hard disk

1 Start DriveSpace.
2 Compress 10 MB of empty space on drive C, creating a new drive J.
3 Start DriveSpace and delete the CVF for the new drive J.

Customize your startup files

1 Create a shortcut to start ScanDisk every time you start Windows 95. (Hint: Use the right mouse button to click the Desktop, then click Create New Shortcut.)
2 Place the shortcut in the StartUp folder.

For more information on	See
Installing a Windows 95 component	Lesson 1
Backing up files on your computer	Lesson 3
Finding and fixing common disk problems	Lesson 3
Optimizing your hard disk	Lesson 3
Compressing your hard disk	Lesson 3
Customizing your startup files	Lesson 2

Step 2: *Set Up a Shared Network Resource*

Because you're working in your home office with a new computer, you want to add the new computer to the network. The network cards and cables have already been installed. Now you'll set up the new computer to share files. You'll also set up the new computer so that each person who logs on to that computer has an individual user profile.

Work with a network server

1 Set up the new computer so that it uses the Client For Microsoft Networks.
2 Set up share-level access.
3 Share drive C as Accounting. Set the Read-Only Password to **readonly**. Set the Full Password to **fullaccess**.

Set up user profiles

1 Turn on user profiles on the computer.
2 Log in as yourself on the computer, change the background color, log off, then log on as Pat Lee.

For more information on	See
Working with a network server	Lesson 4
Setting up user profiles	Lesson 2

Finish the Review & Practice

1 Close all open windows by clicking the Close button.

2 If any window is minimized, use the right mouse button to click the window's taskbar button, and then click Close.

   You are now ready to start the next lesson, or you can work on your own.

3 If you are finished using Windows 95 for now, on the Start menu click Shut Down, and then click Yes.

Part 2

Communicating with Other Computers

Connecting to The Microsoft Network

Estimated time
40 min.

In this lesson you will learn how to:

- Create and modify user accounts.
- View and communicate through bulletin boards.
- Chat with other users of The Microsoft Network.
- Send and receive files.

The Microsoft Network is an online service to which you can connect by using a modem and a phone line. You can use The Microsoft Network to conduct business transactions, communicate with people around the world, and examine information on a variety of topics.

Suppose that your corporate office wants to communicate with you through The Microsoft Network. Your co-workers might need to send you a memo or a budget file, and you might need to send in a travel reimbursement sheet or discuss the new product presentation you're working on. You might join a *chat room*—a special area on The Microsoft Network where you can participate in "live" (*real time*) conversations—to discuss techniques for creating your presentation, and you might want to see whether others have left tips on a bulletin board about creating presentations and speeches. You might also check what's happening around the world by reviewing the news updates on The Microsoft Network. In this lesson, you'll find out how to set up and start using The Microsoft Network with Windows 95.

Creating and Modifying User Accounts

Windows 95 makes it easy to communicate with other computer users through The Microsoft Network. You can send and receive electronic mail (e-mail) and files, talk with other users in chat rooms, browse through bulletin boards, get online information about products and services, and connect to the Internet and various content providers.

In the next exercises, you'll get started by creating and then modifying your user account. Then you'll connect to The Microsoft Network.

Setting Up The Microsoft Network on Your Computer

The first step to using The Microsoft Network is to sign up for service. You must perform two tasks to sign up for The Microsoft Network:

- Install The Microsoft Network component of Windows 95.
- Run The Microsoft Network Signup program.

Install The Microsoft Network component

The Microsoft Network component is not a part of the Typical installation. You must install it separately after you install Windows 95. In this exercise, you install The Microsoft Network component.

1 Click the Start menu, point to Settings, click Control Panel, and then double-click Add/Remove Programs.

2 Click the Windows Setup tab, scroll downward in the list, and then click The Microsoft Network check box if it is not already selected.

3 Click OK.

   The Microsoft Network component is installed. If asked, insert the required CD or disks and click OK.

4 After installing The Microsoft Network, you might need to restart your computer.

Connecting to The Microsoft Network

After you've installed The Microsoft Network component on your computer, you need to run the Signup program to connect to the service. You'll be asked to confirm your personal information as well as to provide a method of billing. (At the time of the writing of this book, The Microsoft Network only supports billing through a major credit card.)

If you've installed The Microsoft Network component on your computer, you're ready to sign up. In the next exercises, you sign up for and connect to The Microsoft Network.

> **IMPORTANT** You will be charged for your use of The Microsoft Network. If you do not want to pay for this service, skip to Lesson 6, "Working with Remote Computers."

Enter your personal information

The Microsoft Network

1   Double-click The Microsoft Network icon on the Desktop.

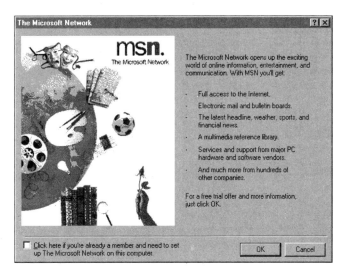

2   Click OK. Then, in The Microsoft Network window, enter your area code and telephone number prefix, and then click OK.

3   Click Connect.

When your system connects to The Microsoft Network, the service transfers the latest setup information. Then the next three windows present the steps you'll need to perform to sign up for The Microsoft Network. The first window asks you for your personal information. Be sure that the information is accurate, because it will be used for sending you billing information. If you don't want your information publicized, you can change your member properties later in this lesson.

4   Click the Tell Us Your Name And Address button, fill out the information, and then click OK.

The next window asks you for a payment method.

5   Click the Next, Select A Way To Pay button, fill out the information, and then click OK.

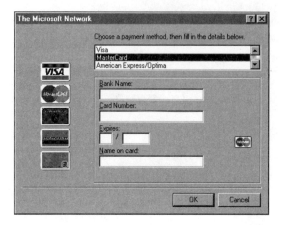

You must select one of four credit cards for payment. If you do not have a credit card account, you cannot sign up for The Microsoft Network. The next window asks you to read the rules for The Microsoft Network.

6   Click the Then, Please Read Rules button, read the information, and then click I Agree.

Now you're ready to connect.

Connect to The Microsoft Network

1   Click the Join Now button, verify that the phone numbers are correct, and then click OK.

The Calling dialog box appears.

2   Click Connect to access The Microsoft Network.

The following dialog box appears.

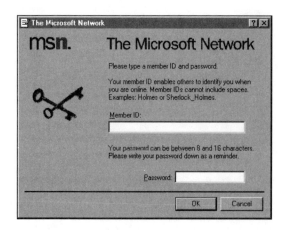

If you forget your password, The Microsoft Network customer service can give you a new password so you can log in to your account.

3 Fill out the Member ID box with a word that you'll use to identify yourself.

Your member ID is used on The Microsoft Network to identify all your transactions. You should pick a member ID that's easy to remember and yet uniquely identifies you. Once you pick a member ID and sign up for The Microsoft Network, you *must* use your ID every time you log on. Your member ID is attached to every transmission you make on The Microsoft Network. You cannot change your member ID. If you decide you do not like your member ID, you must call Customer Service to cancel your account, and then sign up for a new account using a new member ID.

4 Fill out the Password box.

Your password is used on The Microsoft Network to verify your identity. You should not pick a password that can easily be guessed (such as your spouse's or your child's name). Don't use a word that can be found in a dictionary. It's a good idea to use a password with letters, numbers, and other characters, such as 7g@te. Write this password on a piece of paper, and store it in a safe place. If you forget your password, The Microsoft Network will *not* allow you to connect.

You must be using a password to start Windows 95 for the Remember My Password option to be enabled. Use the Passwords icon in Control Panel to set this up.

5 Click Finish. Click the Remember My Password box to place a checkmark in the check box, and fill in the Member ID and Password text boxes.

By clicking here, you won't have to type your password in each time you use The Microsoft Network; however, doing this allows your account to be easily accessed by anyone using your computer.

6 Click Connect to start the sign-up process.

7 After you connect to The Microsoft Network, the taskbar displays an icon for The Microsoft Network.

Viewing Bulletin Boards

Suppose you want to find the latest information on a product, get help on a program you're using, or just discuss an issue with other interested people. You can use a *bulletin board*, or BBS, to post questions, respond to queries, or state your opinion about a topic. A bulletin board is a collection of information that other users have shared on related topics. A bulletin board contains messages that can include objects, such as graphics files or text files, that are part of the messages. Bulletin boards are usually found in *forums*, which are collections of related information on various topics, such as sports or finance.

You view the contents of a bulletin board by opening the bulletin board. Often, each topic on a bulletin board gathers responses from other readers. You can read just the main message, read a response, or browse through the entire collection of the main topic and its responses. This collection is often called a *conversation*.

Open a bulletin board

In this exercise, you open a practice bulletin board in The Microsoft Network.

1 Use the right mouse button to click The Microsoft Network icon in the taskbar.

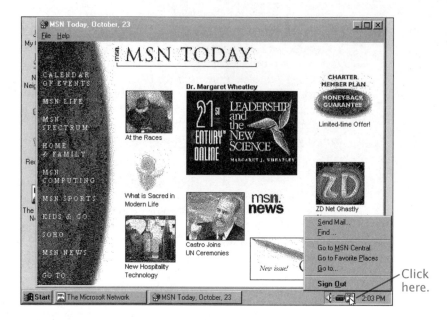

Click here.

You can also click Go To on the MSN Today window, and then click MSN Central.

2 On the shortcut menu, point to Go To MSN Central.

3 In The Microsoft Network window, click Member Assistance.

4 In the Member Assistance window, double-click the Reception Desk forum.

5 Double-click the Practice BBS bulletin board.

The messages in the Practice BBS appear in the window. If this is the first time you've opened this bulletin board, you might have to wait a few moments for all the message titles to appear.

Your screen will not match this illustration. Bulletin boards are dynamic by nature.

Viewing a Message on a Bulletin Board

After you've opened a bulletin board, you can view the messages by opening them.

In the previous exercise, you opened the Practice BBS bulletin board. This bulletin board is set up for new users to practice sending and receiving messages.

Read the messages

In this exercise, you read the messages on the Practice BBS bulletin board.

1 Scroll downward to the first message, and double-click it.

   The message opens.

2 Click the Next Message button.

   The next message appears.

3 Click the Next Message button twice more.

4 Click the Previous Message button.

5 Click the Next Unread Message button.

6 Click the Next Conversation button.

   Be sure that both the Practice BBS window and the topic window are visible so that you can see which conversation you are reading.

7 Click the Previous Conversation button.

8 Click the Next Unread Conversation button.

9 On the message window, click the Close button.

Next Message

Previous Message

Next Unread Message

Creating and Replying to Messages on a Bulletin Board

Next Conversation

After you've viewed a couple of messages and conversations, you might feel ready to post your own message. Posting messages is easy. You can either create a new message, which begins a new conversation, or reply to an existing message.

In either case, you can enter a message of any length. You can format the text of the message to add emphasis.

Previous Conversation

Suppose you have finished reading a message and you want to respond to it. Also, you want to post your own message asking for ideas on creating presentations.

In the next exercises, you reply to a message, and then you create a new message.

Next Unread Conversation

Reply to a message

1 In the BBS window, double-click any message you find interesting.

2 In the window, click the Reply To BBS button.

   The RE: window appears.

Reply To BBS

3 Type **I am interested in more information about presentations**, press ENTER twice, and then type your name.

4 Click the Post Message button.

Post Message

New Message

Compose a message

1 In the BBS window, click the New Message button.

2 In the Subject box, type **SBS Practice Message**

3 Under the Subject box (in the message area), type **Great Expectations**

4 In the message area, type **I am looking for any information about creating and delivering great presentations.**

Your message should look like this:

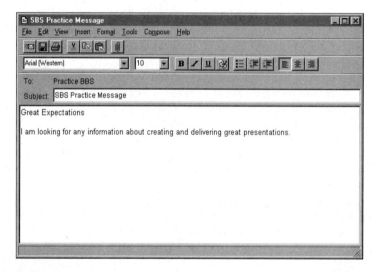

5 Click the Post Message button.

Paste a graphic into a message

Suppose you want to explain your message by including an illustration. You can paste a graphic into your message. When the recipient opens the message, the graphic appears in the message just as it did when you pasted it.

In this exercise, you compose a new message and paste a graphic into it.

1 In the More Windows SBS Practice folder, double-click the Storage folder, and then double-click BBS.bmp.

This is a graphic file you'll paste into a message.

2 On the Edit menu, click Select All.

3   On the Edit menu, click Copy.

The graphic is copied to the Clipboard.

4   On the Paint window, click the Close button.

5   In the BBS window, click the New Message button.

6   In the Subject box, type **SBS Practice Graphic**

7   Under the Subject box (in the message area), type **Here's my picture**.

8   Click in the message area, and on the Edit menu, click Paste.

The graphic is pasted (embedded) into the message. Your message should look like the following illustration.

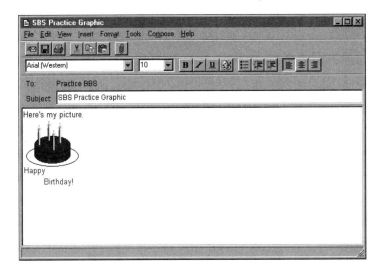

9   Click the Post Message button.

Chatting with Other Users of The Microsoft Network

Suppose you have a question about a product you're using, but you don't want to wait for someone to read your message on a bulletin board and then respond to it. You can use the *chat* feature of The Microsoft Network to talk to other users in *real time,* which means that you see user responses in the chat room window as the responses are typed. You can discuss topics with other Microsoft Network users who are in the same chat room, similar to reading and posting messages on a bulletin board.

The main difference between chat and a bulletin board is that chat is a live session. That is, as soon as you send a message in the chat room, all other users in the same chat room can see your message. Chat rooms can have as few as two users and usually no more than 50. Chat rooms can have *spectators, participants,* and *hosts.* A spectator can view messages but cannot send a message. A participant can both send and view messages. A host controls whether a user is a participant or a spectator.

To begin chatting with other users, you open a chat window.

Opening a Chat Window

Suppose you've decided that you'd like some immediate help on creating presentations. You already posted a message on the Practice BBS bulletin board, but you have some questions you'd like to get answered right away.

Open a chat window

In this exercise, you open a chat window in the MSN Passport forum.

1 In The Microsoft Network window, click Categories, and then double-click MSN Passport. MSN Passport is a central gathering place for international information.

2 Double-click MSN Passport Chat.

The Chat window opens.

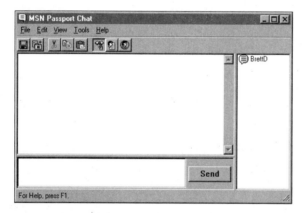

3 Review the ongoing conversation.

4 In the Send box, type a message asking for help on creating presentations, and then press ENTER.

Viewing Member Properties

You might be interested to see who is sending you the replies. You can view the member properties and find out more about the users chatting in the chat room.

Suppose, for example, a user sent you a reply about your question. You appreciate the information, but you'd like to see what background the user has.

View member properties

In this exercise, you view the member properties of a chat room user.

If you are the only member present, you can use your own member name.

1 In the Chat room window, click a member name.

2 On the View menu, click Member Properties.

The Member Properties window appears.

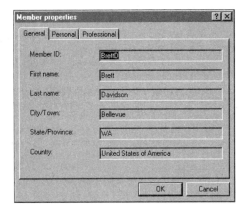

3 Click the Personal tab, and then click the Professional tab.

You can see more about the member properties.

4 Click OK.

Saving a Chat History

Suppose you've been scanning a lively chat session that you want to save. You can copy and paste the information into a text document, of course, but you might find it easier to have the chat room conversations automatically saved.

Save the chat room discussion

In this exercise, you save the contents of the chat room.

1 On the Tools menu, click Options.

2 In the Options window, click the Save Chat History Before Clearing Or Exiting check box to place a checkmark there.

3 Click OK.

4 On the Passport MSN Chat window, click the Close button.

A window appears for you to confirm that you want to save the chat room contents.

109

5 Click Yes.

6 In the File Name box, type **My Chat Room Session** and press ENTER.

The chat room closes. The chat room history (a transcript of the conversation) is saved to the Desktop.

Posting and Downloading Files

One of the benefits of using The Microsoft Network is that you can share files by posting them to a bulletin board. To do this, you compose a message and then attach your file to the message. After you post a file, anyone can copy (download) the file to his or her own computer and then open it. At the end of this section, you'll also learn how to get more information about bulletin boards by using the Help feature in The Microsoft Network.

Post a file to the Practice BBS bulletin board

Suppose your corporate office co-workers would like you to post a file discussing your presentation. Their goal is to have others review the file and post comments.

In this exercise, you compose a message, attach your file to the message, and then post the message file to the Practice BBS bulletin board. The Practice BBS does not show messages with attachments, so you won't see your message on the bulletin board. However, the following procedure can be used to post a file with an attachment to any bulletin board.

1 Open the Practice BBS.

2 On the Compose menu, click New Message.

3 In the Subject box, type **Please review & respond**

4 In the area below the Subject, type **This is a draft of a speech to be presented soon. Can you please review and respond to it? I'd appreciate any input**. Then press ENTER.

You can also insert the contents of a file by choosing the Insert File As Text option.

5 On the Insert menu, click File.

6 Open the Storage folder, click the President's Speech file, and click OK.

The file is attached and appears as an icon in the file.

7 Click the Post button.

Because the content on a bulletin board is monitored, it will usually take a few days before you'll see your message on the bulletin board.

The following is an example of a bulletin board that displays messages with attachments.

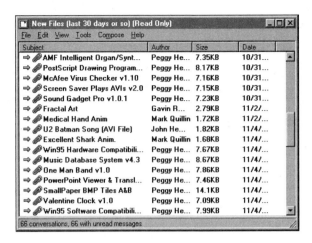

Viewing and retrieving a file

You've probably noticed that other messages on bulletin boards also have the attached file icon. Suppose you've read the messages, and now you want to download the files to your own computer.

In this exercise, you open a message with an attached file and then download the file.

1   Use the right mouse button to click the MSN icon in the taskbar, and then click Go To MSN Central.

2   Click Categories.

3   Double-click Computers And Software, and then double-click Multimedia & CD-ROM.

4   Double-click Multimedia & CD-ROM Forum, and then double-click Multimedia & CD-ROM Library.

5   Double-click New Files (Last 30 Days Or So).

6   Double-click a message that looks interesting to you.

7   Use the right mouse button to click the icon for the attached file, point to File Object, and then click Download.

Get more information on using bulletin boards

In this exercise, you'll learn how you can get more information about using bulletin boards or any other topic related to The Microsoft Network.

1   In The Microsoft Network window on the Help menu, click Help Topics.

The Help Topics: The Microsoft Network Help window appears.

2 Click the Index tab to make it active.

3 In the Type The First Few Letters Of The Word You're Looking For text box, type **BBS**

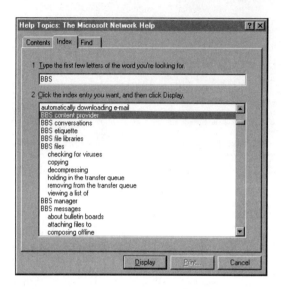

4 Under the heading BBS Files, select the topic Copying, and then click Display.

Whenever a topic has more than one entry, the Topics Found Window will appear as it does here.

5 Double-click the first entry, Copying (Downloading) A File From A Bulletin Board.

The topic window appears with information on copying files from a bulletin board.

6 Read the Help topic and then click the Close button in the Help Topics window.

The window closes and The Microsoft Network screen appears.

Quit The Microsoft Network

1 Use the right mouse button to click The Microsoft Network icon in the taskbar.

2 On the shortcut menu, click Sign Out.

3 Click Yes.

One Step Further: Modifying Your Personal Information on The Microsoft Network

Suppose you've moved to another home, and you want to change your personal information on The Microsoft Network. Maybe you don't want to have some information appear in your personal properties. Or, you might want to add information about your professional affiliations to your properties. You can change the information that appears in your personal properties so that others who view your name can find out more about you.

You use the Address Book to edit your personal properties. Any other user of The Microsoft Network can view your information, but only you can edit it.

In this exercise, you change your Address Book information.

1   Double-click The Microsoft Network icon on the Desktop, and then click Connect.
2   Start Microsoft Exchange.
3   On the Tools menu, click Address Book.
4   Click the down arrow next to Show Names From, and then click Microsoft Network.
5   In the Type Name Or Select From list box, type your first and last name.
6   On the File menu, click Properties.
7   Click the Personal or Professional tab, and change the information.
8   Click OK.
9   When The Microsoft Network Address Book window appears, click OK.
10 Quit The Microsoft Network.

If you want to continue to the next lesson

➤   Close all open windows.

If you want to quit Windows 95 for now

1   Close all open windows.
2   On the Start menu, click Shut Down and then click Yes.

Lesson Summary

To	Do this
Fill out your personal information for The Microsoft Network	Double-click the Signup icon. Fill out the information for your address and your method of payment. Read the rules, and then click OK.
Connect to The Microsoft Network for the first time	Click the Join Now button. Fill out your member ID and password information. Click the Remember My Password box. Click Connect.
Connect to The Microsoft Network for the second and subsequent times	Open The Microsoft Network icon. Click Connect.

To	Do this	Button
Open a bulletin board	Use the right mouse button to click The Microsoft Network icon on the taskbar. Point to Go To MSN Central, open Categories, open a forum, and then open a bulletin board.	
Read a message on a bulletin board	Open the bulletin board, and then open the message.	
Reply to a message	Select the message. In the bulletin board window, click the Reply To BBS button. Fill out your response, and then click the Post button.	
Create a message	In the bulletin board window, click the New Message button. In the Subject box, type a subject. Under the Subject box, type a message, and then click the Post Message button.	
Open a chat window	Open the forum you want to use, and then open the chat room icon you want.	
Send a chat message	Open a chat room. In the Send box, type a message, and then click the Send button.	
View member properties	In a chat room, select a member. On the View menu, click the Member Properties button. Click the Personal or Professional tab. Click OK.	
Save a chat history	Open a chat room. On the Tools menu, click Options. Click Save Chat History Before Clearing Or Exiting. Click OK. In the chat room window, click the Close button. Click Yes. In the File Name box, type a name for the file. Click OK.	
Post a file to a bulletin board	Open the forum, and then open the bulletin board. On the Compose menu, click New Message. In the Subject box, type a subject. In the area below the subject, type a message. On the Insert menu, click File. Open the file you want to send, and click OK. Click the Post button.	

To	Do this
Retrieve a file from a bulletin board	Open a forum, and then open a bulletin board. Open a message that has a paper clip icon attached. Select the icon that represents the attached file. On the Edit menu, point to File Object, and then click Download. Click OK.
Quit The Microsoft Network	Use the right mouse button to click The Microsoft Network icon on the taskbar. Click Sign Out. Click Yes.
Modify your personal information on The Microsoft Network	Connect to The Microsoft Network. Start Microsoft Exchange. In the Microsoft Exchange window, open the Tools menu and click Address Book. Click the down arrow next to Show Names, and select Microsoft Network. In the Type Name Or Select From list box, type your user name. On the File menu, click Properties. Click the Personal or Professional tab, and change the information. Click OK. Click OK again.

For online information about	From The Microsoft Network Help dialog box, click Index and then type
Creating and modifying user accounts	**account, signing up for**
Viewing bulletin boards	**viewing, bulletin board messages**
Chatting with other Microsoft Network users	**chat conversations**
Sending and receiving files on The Microsoft Network	**files, inserting in bulletin board messages**

Preview of the Next Lesson

In the next lesson, you'll communicate with other people using electronic mail. You will compose messages, you'll send them through The Microsoft Network, and then you'll organize the messages into a folder. You can even send messages to online services other than The Microsoft Network, such as Prodigy or America Online.

Communicating with Other Computer Users

Estimated time
40 min.

In this lesson you will learn how to:

- Work with electronic mail in Microsoft Exchange.
- Send and receive messages.
- Paste a file into a message.
- Connect to other mail systems.

Suppose you are working at your home office and need to maintain contact with your corporate office. You can make phone calls to communicate some information, but your department manager also needs to see your detailed responses to some queries. Instead of printing the information and mailing it through the postal service, you can use *Microsoft Exchange*, the electronic messaging manager in Windows 95, to send the mail electronically through the phone lines.

With Microsoft Windows 95, it's easy to communicate with other people using electronic mail. You can compose messages, send them through The Microsoft Network, and organize them in folders. You can even send and receive messages using other mail services.

Working with Electronic Mail in Microsoft Exchange

Microsoft Exchange makes it easy for you to send mail messages to other users. You can use Microsoft Exchange to send mail to recipients who use Microsoft Mail, The Microsoft Network, or other mail systems.

Creating and Sending Mail Messages

To send a message, your computer must be connected to your mail service, usually through a modem and telephone line. You can then send your message with Microsoft Exchange. When you create the mail message, you choose which method Microsoft Exchange will use to send the message. If you're in a corporate office environment where your computer is part of a local area network (LAN), you'll probably use e-mail software, such as Microsoft Mail, Office Vision, or CC:Mail. At your home office, you'll need to use connecting software, such as The Microsoft Network, to send and receive messages.

When you create a message, you type the recipient's mail address. To verify or find a mail address, you can use the Address Book. When your message is complete and correctly addressed, you use Microsoft Exchange to connect to your mail service and send your message.

Create a mail message

In this exercise, you create a mail message using a Microsoft Network mail address. To test how mail works, you'll address the message to yourself.

1   On the Desktop, double-click the Inbox.

    Microsoft Exchange starts.

New Message

2   On the toolbar, click the New Message button.

    A new message window opens.

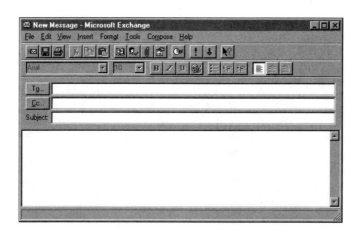

3   In the New Message - Microsoft Exchange window, type your Microsoft Network user name in the To box.

    If you know the address of someone else who is a member of The Microsoft Network, you can use that person's address.

4 In the Subject box, type **Performance Update**

5 In the area below the subject box, type **I've spent some time investigating how we can best work with the Microsoft keyboard. Later this afternoon I'll send you the results of my work.**

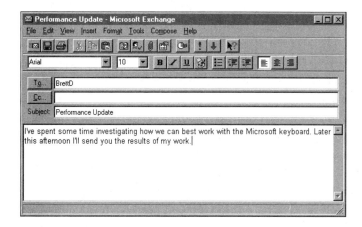

Send the message

Microsoft Exchange can use The Microsoft Network, or another mail service you belong to, to send electronic mail. In this exercise, you send your message by using The Microsoft Network.

Send

1 On the toolbar, click the Send button.

Microsoft Exchange searches for the recipient's name in the Address Book. If the name is found, the message is moved to the Outbox. The next time you connect to your mail service (in this case, The Microsoft Network), the mail will be sent. If the name is not found, the Check Names dialog box will appear. You can use the Address Book to find the correct name, or you can create a new entry for the name. (See the next excercise, "Using the Address Book," for more information.)

2 On the Tools menu, point to Deliver Now Using (or Deliver Now, depending on how many mail services you are using with Microsoft Exchange), and click The Microsoft Network.

Microsoft Exchange starts The Microsoft Network.

3 Click Connect to connect to The Microsoft Network and send your mail.

Microsoft Exchange retrieves any new mail and then disconnects from The Microsoft Network.

NOTE If you are using The Microsoft Network only to send mail, it is cost effective to create your messages while you are not logged onto The Microsoft Network, as you did in the previous exercise. If you plan to use the other features provided by The Microsoft Network, it might be more efficient to first start The Microsoft Network, and then switch to Microsoft Exchange to create and send your messages.

Using the Address Book

Microsoft Exchange provides an online Address Book that you can use to both store and later look up names and addresses of e-mail recipients. If you need to send a message to several people, you can scroll through the Address Book and select all their addresses at once. Or, if you are unsure of the name of someone to whom you want to send a message, you can search for a name in the Address Book.

Depending on whether your computer is standalone or part of a corporate network or LAN, you might have access to multiple Address Books. If you are part of a LAN, there will probably be a Global Address book, that is set up by your network system administrator, and which includes users on your network. If you are connected to The Microsoft Network, you can access The Microsoft Network Address Book. You cannot add names to or delete names from either of these Address Books. You also have a Personal Address Book to which you can add names or copy names from another address book, or from which you can delete names.

Address a message by using your global Address Book

In this exercise, you'll check your recipient's name.

Check Names

This dialog box will also appear if you are sending a message and Microsoft Exchange cannot find the recipient's name.

1   In the New Message window, enter the first one or two letters of a co-worker's name in the To box, and then click the Check Names button on the toolbar.

The Check Names dialog box appears if there is more than one possible name.

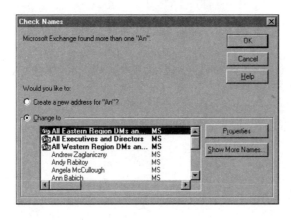

2   In the Change To box, select a name, and then click OK. If no names are listed, click Show More Names to see additional choices.

If your co-worker's name is not listed, you can use the Create A New Address For option to add your co-worker to your Personal Address Book.

3   Click the Close button on the New Message window and then click No.

 NOTE   To have Microsoft Exchange connect to The Microsoft Network to check user names, click Services on the Tools menu, select The Microsoft Network, and then click Properties. On the Address Book tab, click Connect To MSN To Check Names.

Retrieving Mail Messages

In a corporate network environment, Microsoft Exchange checks for new messages frequently if your computer is connected to a LAN. By default, Microsoft Exchange checks for new mail every 10 minutes. You can change this default so that Microsoft Exchange never checks your mail (0 minutes) up to every 9999 minutes (about once a week). You can also check your mail manually, which is the typical method to use when you have only one mail service, such as The Microsoft Network.

Check for mail

In this exercise, you check to see whether you have mail on The Microsoft Network. If you have just completed the previous exercise, Microsoft Exchange has already checked for mail; however, you can try out the following to see how it works.

➤   On the Tools menu, point to Deliver Now Using (or Deliver Now), and click The Microsoft Network.

Microsoft Exchange checks for new mail. If there is any new mail, it is retrieved.

Reading Mail Messages

By default you will see the contents of the Inbox whenever you start Microsoft Exchange.

New mail is placed in the Inbox, which is a folder inside the Personal Folders component of Microsoft Exchange. You open a message to read it. If there are several messages you want to read, you can use the Previous and Next commands to scroll through the messages.

Read and print your mail

1   In the Microsoft Exchange window, click the Inbox folder.

2   Double-click a message to open it so that you can read it.

Print

3   If your computer is connected to a printer, click the Print button on the toolbar to print your message.

4   Click the Close button on the message window to close your message.

TIP You can respond to a mail message you have received. With your mail message open, click Reply To Sender on the Compose menu. Type your reply. Your message is automatically addressed to the sender. Click the Send button on the toolbar to send your message.

Using Folders to Organize Your Mail

Suppose you get many mail messages daily. You can read through the messages, reminding yourself of the information in each, but you might find that you cannot remember what all the messages are about. If you have several messages that you want to save, you can group them according to a common element or topic.

An easy way to keep track of your mail messages is to put them in *folders*. In Microsoft Exchange a folder is a container that you can use to organize your messages and it looks and functions just like any folder you might use in My Computer or Windows Explorer. You can create as many folders as you like. For example, you can create a Projects folder, with three folders inside it: Presentations, Business Documents, and New Employees. Before or after you've read your mail, you can move the messages into the folders. The name of any Microsoft Exchange folder that contains an unread message will be displayed in bold type.

In the following exercises, you create several new folders, change their hierarchical structure, and then move your mail message into a folder.

Create new folders

1 Select the Personal Folders (or Personal Information Store) icon.

2 On the File menu, click New Folder.

3 In the New Folder window, type **Projects** and press ENTER.

4 Select the Projects folder.

5 On the File menu, click New Folder.

6 In the New Folder window, type **Presentations** and press ENTER.

7 Repeat steps 4 through 6 twice, but create a folder named Business Documents and a folder named New Employees.

The folders are created.

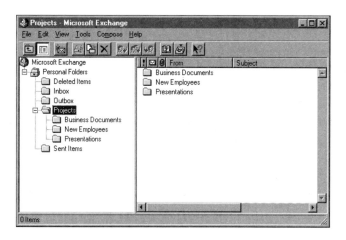

Change the hierarchy of the folders

Suppose you want to move the Business Documents folder so that it is inside the Presentations folder. You can change the hierarchy of the folders by dragging the folders to where you want them.

1 Select the Business Documents folder.

2 Drag it onto the Presentations folder.

A folder inside of another folder is usually referred to as a subfolder.

The Presentations folder now has a plus sign next to it to indicate that it contains one or more folders. The Business Documents folder is now inside of the Presentations folder. This organization helps to reinforce the structure that Business Documents is a subset of Presentations.

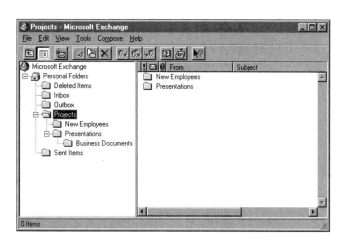

Move a mail message

1   Select the Inbox folder.

2   In the Inbox, select the message that you just read.

3   Drag the message to the Business Documents folder.

4   Open the Business Documents folder.

The message is now in the Business Documents folder.

Deleting Mail Messages

You can delete mail if you do not want to store it for later use. You can delete mail after you read it, or even before you read it. Deleted mail is placed in the Deleted Items folder. However, it is not actually thrown away until you clear the Deleted Items folder. That way, you have a second chance to recover mail that you might accidentally delete. When you clear the Deleted Items folder, the mail that was in it cannot be recovered.

You can change the Microsoft Exchange options so that each time you exit Microsoft Exchange the mail in the Deleted Items folder is automatically thrown away.

In the following exercises, you delete the mail you just moved. Then you clear the Deleted Items folder to throw the mail away. Finally, you change the options in Microsoft Exchange so that items in the Deleted Items folder are automatically thrown away when you exit Microsoft Exchange.

Delete a message

1   In the Microsoft Exchange window, open the Business Documents folder if it is not already open.

2   Select the message you just moved there.

3   On the toolbar, click the Delete button.

The message is moved to the Deleted Items folder.

Delete

Clear the contents of the Deleted Items folder

1   In the Microsoft Exchange window, click the icon for the Deleted Items folder.

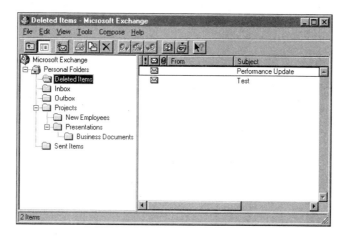

2   Select the message you just moved there.

3   On the toolbar, click the Delete button to permanently delete the message.

Change the Microsoft Exchange options

In this exercise, you change the Microsoft Exchange options for deleted messages.

1   In the Microsoft Exchange window, click Options on the Tools menu.

2   Click the General tab, and then click the Warn Before Permanently Deleting Items check box to remove the checkmark.

3   Click Empty The 'Deleted Items' Folder Upon Exiting to select this option.

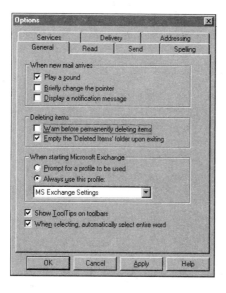

4   Click OK.

Connecting to Other Mail Systems

One of the great benefits of Microsoft Exchange is that you can use it to connect to other mail systems. You can use your personal address book in Microsoft Exchange to store names and addresses of other users so that you don't have to remember their addresses each time you send a note.

You can send messages to users of other online services, such as America Online or CompuServe, or to any user who has access to the Internet (a worldwide interconnection of local area networks), if you know the person's Internet address. An Internet address is in the form *userid@server*, such as Fred@email.com. If you want users to send mail to you on The Microsoft Network by using the Internet, they can send you mail using the form *userid*@msn.com. For example, if your user identification (or user ID) on The Microsoft Network is Plee, then your Internet address would be plee@msn.com.

The following table shows the way to create Internet addresses for various Internet destinations and network service providers.

Service provider or Internet destination	Normal address format	Internet address format
The Microsoft Network	Diogenes	diogenes@msn.com
CompuServe	12345,6789	12345.6789@compuserve.com
Prodigy	Smith2980	smith2980@prodigy.com
America Online	JZwicker02	jzwicker02@aol.com
Delphi	Paula7	paula7@delphi.com
President of the United States		President@whitehouse.gov
Teacher at an educational institution		*instructor@state*.edu
Member of a nonprofit organization		*member@charity*.org

Sending and Receiving Mail Using Internet Addresses

Suppose that you have a consultant, Kelly Miller, who has some information you want to use in your presentation. Kelly, who lives in the next state, has an Internet account. You want to send a message to Kelly. After Kelly reads and responds to the message, you'll receive the return message by the Internet.

In the following exercises, you compose a message to your own user ID as an Internet address on The Microsoft Network. Then you'll send it through Microsoft Exchange. Finally, you'll receive the return message.

Compose an Internet message

New Message

1   In the Microsoft Exchange window, click the New Message button on the toolbar.

2   In the To box, type your Microsoft Network user ID followed by **@msn.com**

3   In the Subject box, type **Request for Information!**

4   In the area below the Subject, type the following text or any other text you like: **Please send me the information you've gathered on creating great presentations!**

5   On the toolbar, click the Send button.

The message is placed in the Outbox.

Send and receive mail via the Internet

Send

If your system is part of a LAN and you have e-mail software, such as Microsoft Mail, your mail will immediately be transferred across the LAN for delivery.

1   On the Tools menu, point to Deliver Now Using (or Deliver Now), and click The Microsoft Network.

Microsoft Exchange begins dialing The Microsoft Network. After your user ID and password are transferred, the message is transferred as well. If you have any new mail, it is downloaded into your Microsoft Exchange Inbox.

2   Wait a few minutes, and then perform Step 1 again.

The Internet might take a few minutes to route your mail to the recipient.

3   When you have waited long enough, your message will appear in your Inbox.

If you send a message to yourself, you might receive your mail as undeliverable. (This is a known problem with The Microsoft Network, which will be fixed as soon as possible.)

One Step Further: Setting Up Microsoft Internet Explorer

Suppose you regularly use the Internet to transmit your mail, and you use the newsgroups and special interest services on the Internet to find information and to conduct research. (A newsgroup is like a bulletin board that provides information about a general topic area.) For example, you might need to send a status report at the end of each day to an associate who uses the Internet, or you might need to check a newsgroup discussing the impact of technology upon working conditions.

By installing an upgraded version of The Microsoft Network (available on The Microsoft Network) that includes an Internet browser, you will have access to all Internet services through Microsoft's Internet Explorer. (An Internet browser does not come with the current retail version of The Microsoft Network software.)

NOTE If you have purchased Microsoft Plus! you already have the Internet Explorer. Go to Lesson 10 for more information on installing the Internet Explorer with Microsoft Plus!

Upgrade The Microsoft Network software

In this exercise, you install the upgraded version of The Microsoft Network, and you set up the Internet Explorer. The installation will place the Internet Explorer icon on your Desktop, and you can use the icon to easily access all the services and information on the Internet.

1 Double-click The Microsoft Network icon.

2 Click Connect.

If others use your computer, it's a good idea to verify your user ID and your password before you connect to The Microsoft Network.

3 When The Microsoft Network window appears, click Categories, and then double-click each of the following to reach The Microsoft Network upgrade:

Computers & Software
Computer Companies & Organizations
Software Companies
Microsoft
The Microsoft Network

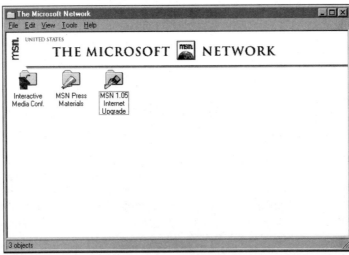

4 Double-click the MSN v1.05 Internet Upgrade folder, and then double-click the Upgrade To The Microsoft Network Software icon.

The upgrade is downloaded to your computer. This process will probably take several minutes to complete.

Quit and restart The Microsoft Network

In this exercise, you restart The Microsoft Network to use the upgraded software.

1   On the taskbar, use the right mouse button to click The Microsoft Network icon, and then click Sign Out.

2   On the Desktop, double-click The Microsoft Network icon.

3   Click Connect, and then click OK.

4   Select a phone number, and click OK.

5   After you connect to The Microsoft Network, you have access to the Internet.

If you want to continue to the next lesson

➤   Close all open windows.

If you want to quit Windows 95 for now

1   Close all open windows.

2   On the Start menu, click Shut Down.

3   Click Shut Down The Computer? and then click Yes.

Lesson Summary

To	Do this	Button
Create a mail message	Start Microsoft Exchange. Click the New Message button. Type an address, type a subject, and then type the message.	
Send a mail message through The Microsoft Network	In Microsoft Exchange, create a new mail message. Click the Send button. On the Tools menu, point to Deliver Now Using (or Deliver Now), and then click The Microsoft Network. When The Microsoft Network dialog box appears, click Connect.	
Retrieve a mail message from The Microsoft Network	Open The Microsoft Network. Switch to Microsoft Exchange. From the Tools menu, point to Deliver Now Using (or Deliver Now), and then click The Microsoft Network.	

To	Do this	Button
Read a mail message	In Microsoft Exchange, select a message and double-click it.	
Create folders to organize messages	In Microsoft Exchange, select the Personal Information Store. On the File menu, click New Folder. Type a folder name, and press ENTER.	
Move a message to a folder	In Microsoft Exchange, select the message you want to move, and then drag it to another folder.	
Delete a mail message	In Microsoft Exchange, select the message, and then click the Delete button.	
Clear the Deleted Items folder	In Microsoft Exchange, open the Deleted Items folder. On the Edit menu, click Select All. On the File menu, click Delete.	
Automatically clear the Deleted Items folder whenever you exit Microsoft Exchange	In Microsoft Exchange, click Options on the Tools menu. Click General, and then click Warn Before Permanently Deleting Items to remove the checkmark. Click Empty The 'Deleted Items' Folder Upon Exiting to place a checkmark in the check box. Click OK.	

For online information about	From the Microsoft Exchange Help Topics dialog box, click Index and then type
Creating and sending mail messages	**composing messages**
Using folders	**folders**

Preview of the Next Lesson

In the next lesson, you'll learn to send and receive files without using an online service such as The Microsoft Network. You'll also learn how to send and receive faxes.

Lesson

7

Working with Remote Computers

Estimated time
40 min.

In this lesson you will learn how to:

■ Connect to a network using a remote computer.

■ Send and receive faxes.

With Microsoft Windows 95, it's easy to connect to other computers. You can send and receive files without using an online service such as The Microsoft Network, and you can also send and receive faxes. In this lesson, you learn how to connect to a network using a remote computer, and how to send and receive faxes.

Connecting to a Network Through a Remote Computer

Suppose you've been working at your home office for several weeks, and you have a few files that you'd like to update on the network server at the corporate office. Although the server at the corporate office is connected to a modem, it does not have access to any online service, so you can't send the file using such a service. (For more information on network servers, see Lesson 4, "Working with Network Resources.")

NOTE   The term "remote computer" can refer to either your computer or the computer to which you want to connect that is back at the corporate office. Typically, however, the remote computer is the one that has to use a phone line to initiate a Remote connection.

You'd like to get the files to the network server at the corporate office as quickly as possible. What can you do? With Windows 95, it's easy to connect two computers together using *Dial-Up Networking*. With Dial-Up Networking, you can make a remote connection to a standalone computer, a computer connected to a network, or even a network server. You can also use any printer or fax modem that the computer you are connecting to can access. You can print your documents, transfer files, create new files and folders, and do most anything else you can do when you are working on a computer at the corporate office.

There are several steps to making a remote connection to another computer. You must select

- A dial-up client and a server
- A remote access protocol
- A network (LAN) protocol and network server
- Security options

The *dial-up client* is your computer that calls into the remote server. (The remote server must be using a compatible operating system or network operating system, such as Windows 95, Windows NT 3.1 or greater, Windows for Workgroups, or NetWare Connect.) The *remote access protocol* controls how data is transmitted, and both the dial-up client and the remote server must be using the same protocol. The *network protocol* is used if you are connecting through the remote server to your network. The *security options*, set by the network administrator located at your corporate office, determine what level of access you have to the network, computers, and other resource that are at the corporate office.

 NOTE To connect to a remote network, you must dial-up to a computer or server that supports a remote connection. For more information about setting up a computer to support a remote connection, see Lesson 11.

Installing Dial-Up Networking

Let's say that your corporate office has recently upgraded its network system to allow dial-up access. To take advantage of this new service, you want to install Dial-Up Networking on your home computer so that you can call the corporate office, transfer files, and then print documents on a network printer located at the corporate office.

You might have already installed support for Dial-Up Networking, if you chose the Custom installation when you first installed Windows 95. If not, you can add Dial-Up Networking support using the Add/Remove Programs icon in Control Panel.

Install Dial-Up Networking

In this exercise, you install support for Dial-Up Networking on your computer.

1   Click the Start button, point to Settings, and then click Control Panel.

If there is a checkmark in the box next to the Dial-Up Networking component, it is already installed on your computer. You don't need to install it again.

2 Double-click the Add/Remove Programs icon, and then click the Windows Setup tab.

3 Click Communications, and then click the Details button.

4 Click Dial-Up Networking, click OK, and then click OK again.

Windows 95 installs the Dial-Up Networking component. You might be prompted to insert the Windows 95 setup disks or CD-ROM.

5 On the Control Panel window, click the Close button.

TROUBLESHOOTING If there is a checkmark next to any Windows 95 component in the Add/Remove Programs dialog box, but you are not able to access that component, you might have inadvertently deleted it through My Computer or Windows Explorer. To have Windows 95 reinstall it properly, you can remove the checkmark next to the component, click Apply, place the checkmark next to the component again, and then click OK. Windows 95 will then install the component.

Calling a Remote Computer

Now that you've set up Dial-Up Networking support, you're ready to call your corporate office. You'll need to know the remote access phone number for your corporate office, including the area code and country code, and the description of the modem with which you're using to make the call.

Remote Connection

Information, such as the phone number, supported protocols, modem type and settings, and name of the remote connection, is stored in a file. The file is stored in the Dial-Up Networking folder. Double-clicking the Remote Connection icon (shown at left) opens the file and starts the procedure to establish the remote connection.

NOTE You must install support for your modem before you can use Dial-Up Networking. If you've connected a modem but have not installed support for it when you start Dial-Up Networking, the Make New Connection wizard will prompt you to set up your modem before creating a new connection.

In the next exercises, you set up a remote connection using the Make New Connection wizard. Then you call the remote computer.

Make a new connection

1 Click the Start button, point to Programs, point to Accessories, and then click Dial-Up Networking.

Make New Connection

You can also double-click My Computer, and then double-click Dial-Up Networking, and then double-click Make New Connection.

2 Double-click the Make New Connection icon.

The Make New Connection wizard appears.

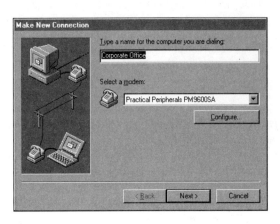

3 In the Type A Name For The Computer You Are Dialing box, type **Corporate Office**

If you have more than one modem connected to your computer you can click the down arrow button to select from a list of installed modems.

4 Verify that the modem description in the Select A Modem box describes one that is connected to your computer and is the one you want to use, and then click Next.

5 In the Area Code box, type the area code for the computer you want to connect to and in the Telephone number box, type the telephone number for that computer, and then click Next.

Your screen should look similar to the following.

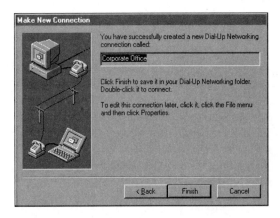

6 Click Finish.

The new dial-up connection appears in the Dial-Up Networking window.

Establish the remote connection

1 In the Dial-Up Networking window, double-click the Corporate Office icon.

The user name and password will have been set up by the administrator of the remote server or computer.

2 Verify that the text in the User name box is correct. In the Password box, type the remote access password, and then click Connect. If this is the first time you've connected, a window might appear for you to confirm the name of the remote server as well as the password for the server.

3 If necessary, in the Password box, type your password for the remote server, confirm the name of the remote server, and then click OK.

The connection is established.

Working with Resources on the Remote Server

Suppose you have a file on your local computer that you'd like to transfer to the corporate office. You'd also like to print a file to the high quality laser printer at the corporate office. If your computer is connected to the remote server and you have the necessary access rights (predetermined privileges for your user name that have been established by the administrator of the remote server), you can transfer, create, delete, edit, and print your files.

Now that your computer is connected to the remote server, you can easily work with its resources (disks, files, folders, printers, and so on), just as if your local computer were right there at the corporate office. You can transfer files between your computer and the remote computer, print to any printer connected to the remote computer, create and delete files and folders, start programs, send and receive e-mail, and even use a fax modem (much like you use a printer) on the remote computer (if there is one and it is set up to be shared by other users).

In the next exercises, you transfer a file to the remote computer, you set up a remote printer, and then you print a file on the remote printer.

Transfer a file

1 Double-click Network Neighborhood, and then double-click the remote computer icon.

 TIP If you do not see the remote computer icon in the Network Neighborhood window, click Start, point to Find, and then click Computer. Type the name of the remote computer, and then click Find Now.

2 Double-click a folder on the remote computer, and then, on the Network Neighborhood window, click the Minimize button.

3 On the C drive of your computer double-click the More Windows SBS Practice folder, and then double-click the Exercise folder.

4 Drag the Presentation Budget file from the Exercise folder to the folder on the remote computer.

The file is copied to the remote computer.

5 On the Exercise window, click the Close button.

6 On the remote computer's folder, click the Close button.

Set up a remote printer

1 Double-click Network Neighborhood, and then double-click the remote computer.

2 Double-click a printer attached to the remote computer.

Since your computer needs to know how the remote printer works, you are asked to set up the remote.

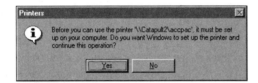

3 Click Yes.

Unlike MS-DOS, Windows 95 can print directly to a networked or remote printer without using a port such as LPT1. To assign the printer to a port, click Yes.

4 For simplicity, click No to disable printing from MS-DOS–based programs, and then click Next.

5 Click the brand name and model of the remote printer, and then click Next.

6 Type a name for the printer that will help you remember what kind of printer it is and where it's located, and then click Next.

The setup files are either copied from the remote computer or from your Windows 95 setup disks to your computer (you'll be prompted to insert the CD-ROM or disks if necessary). If you already have a printer driver of the same model set up on your machine, you'll be prompted to use the existing driver or overwrite the existing driver with the new one.

7 Since you won't be able see the test results, when asked to print a test page, click No, and then click the Finish button.

8 After the printer driver files are copied, click OK.

The remote printer is now set up for use on your computer.

9 On the Network Neighborhood window, click the Close button.

In the next exercise, you create a shortcut to the printer that you just set up. This will allow you to just drag a file's icon to the shortcut to print the file.

Create a shortcut for the remote printer

1 Click the Start menu, point to Settings, and then click Printers.

2 Drag the new printer icon you just defined to the Desktop, and then click Yes.

A shortcut for the remote printer is created.

3 On the Printers window, click the Close button.

Print a file on a remote printer

1 On the Desktop, double-click the Exercise folder.

2 Drag the Presentation Budget file to the remote printer Shortcut icon.

The local file is printed on the remote printer.

3 On the Exercise folder, click the Close button.

Sending and Receiving Faxes

Faxes (or facsimiles) are a standard feature of most offices, whether at the corporate location or at home. Most contemporary modems are capable of sending and receiving faxes as well as traditional data communications.

Suppose, for example, that your corporate office wants you to submit a daily report on your activities. You could send them a file using Dial-Up Networking or e-mail, or you could print the report on the remote printer; but for this kind of task it is usually easier just to send a fax from your computer to their fax machine. There are several advantages of faxing a file instead of using Dial-Up Networking or e-mail. For example, the fax can be scheduled to be sent at a specific time, unattended. It takes far less time to fax a file than it does to log on to a remote computer, transfer or print the file and then log off. And e-mail can vary from one day to the next in the amount of time it takes to transfer data.

You use Microsoft Exchange to send and receive faxes. You can send faxes from any program that lets you print documents. Instead of printing to a printer, however, you can print to your fax modem. Microsoft Exchange takes care of scheduling and transmitting the fax.

Configuring Fax Hardware and Software

Suppose you've recently purchased a modem that can send and receive faxes. You didn't have a fax modem when you installed Windows 95, so now you need to install the Microsoft Fax component, and then install the Microsoft Fax service in Microsoft Exchange. After you set up the basic information for faxing, you can send and receive faxes using Microsoft Exchange.

You must configure your fax modem before you can use it to send and receive faxes. There are several steps required to configure a fax modem.

- Install the Microsoft Fax component.
- Add the Microsoft Fax service.
- Specify the fax information.

The Microsoft Fax component can be installed either at the time you install Windows 95 or later. After you've installed the Microsoft Fax component, you can add the Microsoft Fax service to Exchange.

In the next exercises, you install the Microsoft Fax component and then add the Microsoft Fax service.

Install the Microsoft Fax component

If you already have installed the Microsoft Fax component, you can skip to the next exercise.

1 Click the Start menu, point to Settings, and then click Control Panel.

2 Double-click the Add/Remove Programs icon, and then click the Windows Setup tab.

3 Click the check box next to Microsoft Fax to place a checkmark, and then click OK.

This selects the Microsoft Fax component, which consists of the Microsoft Fax service and the Microsoft Fax Viewer. When you click OK, you might be asked to insert a Windows 95 disk or CD-ROM.

Add the Microsoft Fax service

1 Click the Start button, point to Settings, and then click Control Panel. In the Control Panel window, double-click the Mail And Fax icon.

The Mail And Fax window appears.

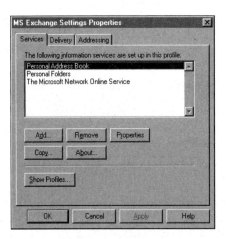

2 Click the Services tab, and then click the Add button.

3 Click Microsoft Fax, and click OK.

You are asked to specify the information used to send faxes.

4 Click Yes.

The Microsoft Fax Properties window appears.

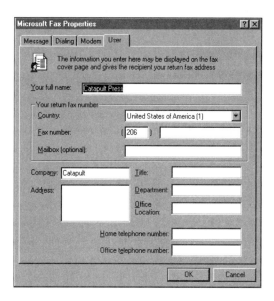

5 Fill out the personal information on the page, and then click the Modem tab.

This information will be displayed in the cover page.

6 Select the modem you want to use for your fax, and then click the Set As Active Fax Modem button.

Modifying and Using a Fax Cover Page

Since you're going to send a fax (in this case, the Keyboard Information file) to your corporate office, you'll want to identify who gets the fax. You'll attach a cover page to identify the contents of the fax as well as the recipient and the sender. The cover page is the first page sent of a fax. This page usually contains the information that identifies the recipient of the fax, the subject of the fax, and any additional data you'd like to send to help route the fax to the appropriate person.

Now that you've installed the Microsoft Fax component and the Microsoft Fax service, you're ready to create a fax. You can use one of the four fax cover pages (if you installed Windows 95 from floppy disks there'll only be one fax cover page), or you can edit the contents and layout of an existing fax cover page to create a new cover page.

In the next exercises, you'll modify a fax cover page and then use it when sending a fax.

Modify a fax cover page

1 In the Microsoft Fax Properties window, click the Message tab.

2 In the Default Cover Page area, click Generic, and then click the Open button.

The Cover Page Editor window appears, with the Cover Page Editor Tips window.

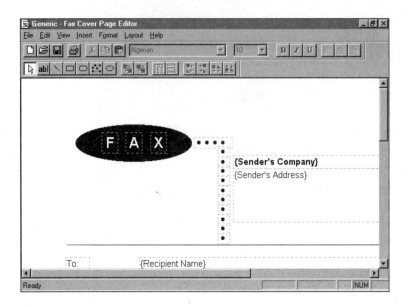

3 Click OK.

4 In the Cover Page Editor window, click the Maximize button.

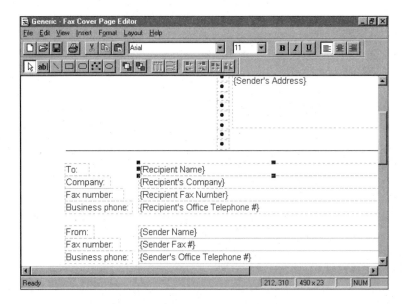

5 On the File menu, click Save As.

6 In the File Name box, type **My Cover Page**, and then press ENTER.

7   Click the Sender's Company field, hold down CTRL, and then click the Sender's Address field.

This selects both fields in the fax cover page.

8   Click the Font down arrow, and then click Times New Roman.

9   Click the Font Size down arrow, and then click 14.

The text for the selected fields in the cover page is changed. Your screen looks like this.

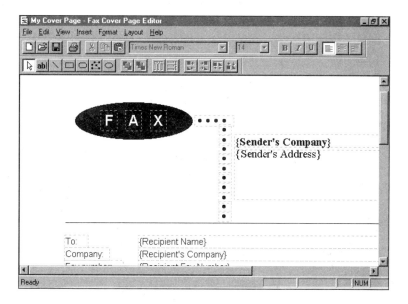

10   On the File menu, click Save, and then on the My Cover Page - Fax Cover Page Editor window click the Close button.

11   In the Microsoft Fax Properties dialog box, click OK.

Create a fax

1   In the More Windows SBS Practice folder, double-click the Exercise folder, and then double-click the Keyboard Information icon.

2   On the File menu, click Print.

3   Click the down arrow in the Name box, and then click Microsoft Fax.

4   Click OK.

WordPad (or Microsoft Word, if it's installed on your computer) begins printing the fax. Then the fax service presents the Compose New Fax window for you to confirm the location and telephone number for the fax.

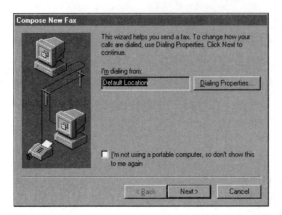

5 Click Next. In the To box, type the recipient's name. Then, in the Fax # box, type the fax telephone number for the recipient.

6 Verify the information, click the Add To List button, and then click Next.

7 Under Do You Want To Send A Cover Page?, click Yes, click My Cover Page, and then click Next.

If you have set a specific delivery time, the fax will be placed in the Outbox of Microsoft Exchange.

8 In the Subject box, type **Attached is the information you requested.** In the Note box, type **Here's all the information on the new Microsoft Natural Keyboard you requested. Let me know if you need more information.** Click the Start Note On Cover Page box, and then click Next.

9 Click Finish.

The fax is sent to its destination.

Receiving and Forwarding Faxes

Now that you have sent a fax, you'll learn how to receive faxes using Microsoft Exchange. Since Microsoft Exchange handles the transmission of faxes, you can specify the time to send and receive faxes. After receiving a fax, you can then forward it to someone else.

In the next exercises, you receive and then forward a fax. You'll need to have someone send you a fax to complete this exercise. If you don't have someone who can send you a fax you can use a fax service such as Microsoft FastTips. Microsoft FastTips is available 7 days a week 24 hours a day by calling (800) 936-4100. Microsoft FastTips provides answers to common technical problems and a catalog of available information on a variety of topics. Respond to the recorded prompts with your touch tone phone to request a fax.

Receive a fax

1 On the Desktop, double-click the Inbox, if Microsoft Exchange is not already running.

2 On the Tools menu, point to Deliver Now Using, and then click Microsoft Fax.

If the Modem status message box does not appear, double click the icon of the fax machine in the taskbar, next to the clock.

3 If you have not set up your fax modem to answer the phone automatically, click Answer Now in the Microsoft Fax Status dialog box.

When the modem answers, Microsoft Exchange will receive the fax and place it in your Inbox.

If you are working where there's only one phone line, you probably do not want your fax modem to automatically answer the phone.

Forward

Forward a fax

1 Select the fax you just received, and then click the Forward button.

2 In the User Name box, type a name of someone you want to forward the fax to. Then, in the Phone number box, type that person's phone number.

3 Click the Add To List button, and then click Next.

You can add several recipient names to the To list, and Microsoft Exchange will take care of dialing each one in turn and sending the fax.

4 Click Next, click No, and then click Finish.

Reading, Printing, and Deleting a Fax

Suppose you've received a fax from your corporate office regarding your research on Microsoft's Natural Keyboard. After reading it, you decide to keep a paper copy and then delete the electronic file.

Faxes are stored in the Microsoft Exchange Inbox in the same way as your other mail. You can read, print, and delete faxes as easily as mail.

In the next exercises, you read a fax, print it, and then delete it.

Read the fax

1 Double-click the fax that was sent to you.

2 Scroll through the fax to read it.

3 On the fax window, click the Close button.

Print the fax

1 Click the fax that was sent to you.

2 Click the Print button.

The fax is printed.

Print

Delete the fax and close Microsoft Exchange

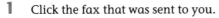

1 Click the fax that was sent to you.

2 Click the Delete button.

The fax is deleted.

Delete

3 On the Exchange window, click the Close button.

Exchange closes.

One Step Further: Adding a Shortcut to the Send To Menu

You can make it easy to transfer files to a remote computer by creating a shortcut for the Send To menu. For example, you might want to send a budget file to your corporate office, but you don't want to have to locate and open the desired folder, and then drag your file to the Send To window each time you want to transfer a file. Creating a shortcut in the Send To menu can save you time.

In the next exercises, you add a shortcut to the Send To menu, and then send a file to your corporate office.

Create the shortcut

1 Click the Start menu, point to Programs, click Accessories, click Dial Up Networking, and then click Corporate Office.

2 Click OK, and then connect to the corporate office.

3 On your Desktop, open My Computer, open the Drive C icon, open Windows, and then open Send To.

4 Use the right mouse button to drag any folder from the Corporate Office window to the Send To window.

5 Click Create Shortcut Here.

6 Close all open folder windows.

Use the shortcut to transfer a file

1 Open the More Windows SBS folder and then open the Exercise folder.

2 Use the right mouse button to click the Budget Report file.

If your computer is not connected to the corporate office, Dial-Up Networking will first establish a connection.

3 On the shortcut menu point to Send To, and then click the folder name that references the one at the corporate office.

The file is copied to the folder on the computer at the corporate office.

4   On the Exercise folder window, hold down the SHIFT key and then click the Close button.

5   On the Dial-Up Networking connection window, click the Close button.

If you want to continue to the next lesson

➤   Close all open windows.

If you want to quit Windows 95 for now

1   Close all open windows.

2   On the Start menu, click Shut Down.

3   Click Shut Down The Computer? and then click Yes.

Lesson Summary

To	Do This
Install Dial-Up Networking on your computer	Click the Start menu, point to Settings, and then click Control Panel. Open Add/Remove Programs, and then click the Windows Setup tab. Click Communications, and then click Details. Click Dial-Up Networking, click OK, and then click OK again.
Make a new connection to a remote computer	Click the Start menu, point to Programs, point to Accessories, and then click Dial-Up Networking. Double-click Make New Connection. Type a name for the connection, and click Next. Type a phone number for the connection, and click Next. Click Finish.
Connect to a remote computer	In the Dial-Up Networking window, open the connection. Click Connect. Type your password, if necessary, and then click OK.
Transfer a file to a remote computer	Open Network Neighborhood, and then connect to the remote computer. Connect to a local folder. Drag a file from the local folder to the remote computer.

To	Do This
Set up a remote printer	Open Network Neighborhood, and then connect to the remote computer. Connect to a remote printer, and then click OK. Click No, and then click Next. Identify the printer name and model, and then click Next. Type a name for the printer, and click Next. Click No, and then click Finish.
Install the Microsoft Fax component	Click the Start menu, point to Settings, and then click Control Panel. Double-click the Add/Remove Programs icon, and then click the Windows Setup tab. Click the check box next to Microsoft Fax, and then click OK.
Add the Microsoft Fax service	In the Control Panel window, double-click the Mail And Fax icon. Click the Services tab, and then click the Add button. Click Microsoft Fax, and click OK. Click OK. Fill out the information, and click the Modem tab. Click the name of your modem, and then click the Set As Active Fax button.
Modify a fax cover page	In the Microsoft Fax Properties window, click the Message tab. In the Default Cover Page area, click Generic, and click Open. Click OK. On the File menu, click Save As, type a name, and then click OK. Make the changes you want, and then, on the File menu, click Save. On the Cover Page Editor Window, click the Close button.
Create a fax	Open a document in a Windows 95 program. On the File menu, click Print. Click the Name down arrow, and then click Microsoft Fax. Click Next, type the recipient's name, type the fax - phone number, click the Add To List button, and then click Next. Click Yes, click the cover page, and then click next. Type a subject and note. Click Next, and then click Finish.

To	Do This	Button
Send a fax	Open the Inbox. On the Tools menu, point to Deliver Now Using, and click Microsoft Fax.	
Receive a fax	Open the Inbox. On the Tools menu, point to Microsoft Fax Tools, and click Receive Fax Now.	
Forward a fax	Open the Inbox. Click the fax, and then click the Forward button.	
Read a fax	Click the fax, and press ENTER.	
Print a fax	Click the fax, and click the Print button.	
Delete a fax	Click the fax, and then click the Delete button.	

For online information about	From the Help dialog box, click Index and then type
Installing Dial-Up Networking	**Dial-Up Networking, installing**
Calling a remote computer	**calling another computer, by using Dial-Up Networking**
Working with remote resources	**printer drivers, installing**
Sending and receiving faxes	**fax, exchanging faxes**
Configuring fax hardware and software	**fax, installing Microsoft Fax**

Preview of the Next Lesson

In the next lesson, you'll learn how to play sound files, such as waveform files or MIDI files. You'll learn how to record sounds and then how to assign them to Windows 95 events, such as the start of a program. And, you'll learn how to play multimedia files, which can contain any combination of animations, video, pictures, sounds, or text.

Review & Practice

In the lessons in Part 2, you learned skills to help you connect with other computers through such means as The Microsoft Network, electronic mail, Dial-Up Networking, and sending faxes. If you want to practice these skills and test your understanding before you proceed with the lessons in Part 3, you can work through the Review & Practice section following this lesson.

Review & Practice

You will review and practice how to:

Estimated time
25 min.

■ Set up The Microsoft Network.
■ Post messages to a bulletin board.
■ Send and receive electronic mail.
■ Connect to a remote computer.
■ Send and receive faxes.

You can practice the skills you learned in Part 2 by working through the steps in this Review & Practice session. You'll use The Microsoft Network to send and receive e-mail, and to post messages a bulletin board. You'll connect to a remote computer to send a file, and you'll use Microsoft Exchange to send a fax.

Scenario

Now that you have successfully set up one computer in your home office, you're ready to set up an additional computer. Because of the increase in the amount of information you must transmit to your co-workers, your corporate office has approved your request to use The Microsoft Network. You'll set up The Microsoft Network on your additional computer using your existing user name and password. Then you'll use the capabilities of The Microsoft Network to send and receive electronic mail and faxes, post messages, and send a file to a remote computer.

Step 1: Set Up The Microsoft Network

In this step, you'll set up The Microsoft Network on a computer. First you'll install The Microsoft Network component. Then you'll log onto The Microsoft Network and sign up as an existing user. Because you're already signed on as a user, you can customize The Microsoft Network manually.

1 Install The Microsoft Network component from Windows 95.

2 Start The Microsoft Network.

3 In the first window, click the Click Here If You're Already A Member And Need To Set Up The Microsoft Network On This Computer box, and then click OK.

Because you signed up for The Microsoft Network earlier in these lessons, you don't need to choose a new user name. You can use your existing user name.

4 Set up your phone number.

5 In the Member ID box, type your user name. In the Password box, type your password, and then click Connect.

For more information on	See
Installing The Microsoft Network	Lesson 5

Step 2: Post a Message to a Bulletin Board

In this step, you'll create a message for a bulletin board, and then you'll post it.

1 On The Microsoft Network, open MSN Central and then open Member Assistance.

2 Open the Reception Desk Practice BBS.

3 Create a message with the title **Information About Home Offices** and the following text:

I'm looking for any information about connecting a home office to the corporate office.

4 Post your message.

5 Close the MSN Central window, and disconnect from The Microsoft Network.

For more information on	See
Posting a message to a bulletin board	Lesson 5

Step 3: Send and Receive Electronic Mail

In this step, you'll create a new message in Microsoft Exchange. Then you'll send it using The Microsoft Network.

Send electronic mail

1 Connect to The Microsoft Network and then click Electronic Mail.

2 Create a message to yourself on The Microsoft Network.

3 Send your mail using The Microsoft Network.

Receive electronic mail

1 Wait about 5 or more minutes, and then check your mail. (Hint: Use the Deliver Now Using command on the Tools menu.)

2 Use the MSN icon on the taskbar to disconnect from The Microsoft Network.

For more information on	See
Creating mail	Lesson 6
Sending mail	Lesson 6
Receiving mail	Lesson 6

Step 4: Connect to a Remote Computer

In this step, you'll install dial-up networking support. Then you'll connect to a remote computer. Finally, you'll send a file to the remote computer.

 NOTE To do this step, you must have access to a remote computer that supports dial-up networking and can accept transferred files.

Install Dial-Up Networking

1 Open the Control Panel.

2 Use the Add/Remove Programs icon to add support for dial-up networking.

3 Close the Control Panel.

Call a remote computer

1 Start Dial-Up Networking.

2 Use the Add New Connection icon to create a new connection to a friend's computer.

3 Connect to your friend's computer.

Transfer a file to the remote computer

1 Open the More Windows SBS Practice folder.
2 Send the Business file to the remote computer.
3 Close the remote connection.
4 Close the My Computer and Dial-Up Networking windows.

For more information on	See
Installing Dial-up Networking	Lesson 7
Calling a Remote Computer	Lesson 7
Transferring a File to a Remote Computer	Lesson 7

Step 5: *Create and Send a Fax*

1 Start Microsoft WordPad or Word and create a new document. Print the document using Microsoft Fax as your printer.
2 In the Compose New Fax wizard, type the requested information. Click Next until the subject text box appears in the wizard.
3 Type **Information About Home Offices Wanted** for the subject, and type the following text for a message:

   I am looking for more information about setting up a home office.

4 Send the fax using Microsoft Exchange.

For more information on	See
Creating a fax	Lesson 7
Sending a fax	Lesson 7

Finish the Review & Practice

1 Close all open windows by clicking the Close button.
2 If any window is minimized, use the right mouse button to click the window's taskbar button, and then click Close.

   You are now ready to start the next lesson, or you can work on your own.

3 If you are finished using Windows 95 for now, on the Start menu click Shut Down, and then click Yes.

Using Multimedia Files

Part 3

Working with Multimedia Files

In this lesson you will learn how to:

- Set up sound support.
- Play and record sound files.
- Use the Media Player to play multimedia files.

Multimedia combines sound, graphics, animation, video, or text, to create a dynamic mix of images and data. Windows 95 provides some basic tools to get started with multimedia. These include basic audio recording, and audio and video playback. With these tools, you can create sound files to include in your documents or assign to Windows 95 actions (called *events*). You can also play commercial audio or multimedia CDs that provide an exciting array of information and entertainment.

A basic multimedia system will include an SVGA 16-bit monitor, a 16-bit audio sound card with MIDI support, and a double-speed CD-ROM drive. A multitude of multimedia components are available to add to these basics, depending on your budget and your needs.

This lesson provides an introduction into the basic multimedia tools provided with Windows 95. You'll set up sound support and the Media Player so you can play multimedia files. You'll play different types of sound files, and you'll record some sounds. You'll even assign a sound to a Windows 95 event.

Setting Up Sound Support

Sound can make a computer-based presentation into a memorable experience. For example, you can add voice notes to your documents so that your reader can hear what you have to say.

Suppose that you want to add some recorded sounds to a presentation you're developing. You might want to have a dramatic theme song play when your presentation starts, and then have a soft musical interlude play during another part of the presentation. You might also want to have your own narration play during portions of the presentation.

Before you can play or record sounds, you must install a *sound card*. The sound card includes the interface card that connects to your computer. After you install the sound card, you can install the speakers to play the sounds. (The speaker in a computer isn't usually good enough to play sounds well.) You can also purchase a microphone and a set of earphones to use with the sound card.

After you install the sound card, you must install the *driver* needed to support the sound card. The driver is the software that Windows 95 uses to run the device and play or record sound.

Installing a Sound Card

Most new computers come with a sound card already installed. If your computer does not have a sound card, installing a Plug-and-Play–compatible sound card is straightforward. Plug and Play lets you add new devices to your computer without performing a lengthy and complicated configuration of the device. Usually you simply plug the sound card into an interface slot on the motherboard of your computer. Windows 95 will use Plug and Play to detect the new device and install the driver. If Windows 95 is unable to load the driver, you can manually install it. (See Lesson 1, "Setting Up Your Computer," for more information about using Plug and Play.)

If your sound card is not Plug-and-Play compatible, you can install and configure it successfully with the Add Hardware Wizard. See Lesson 1, "Setting Up Your Computer," for more information about using the Add Hardware Wizard. If your sound card is not Plug-and-Play–compatible, and the Add Hardware Wizard doesn't install it correctly, you might need to use the software supplied with the sound card.

 WARNING   The internal components of your computer are very sensitive to static electricity. If you are not experienced with installing computer devices, it is recommended that you have a qualified service professional install the sound card for you.

Install a sound card

This exercise is a brief overview that describes how to install a sound card. Some of the steps involve more detail than can be discussed in this book, and they assume that you have some familiarity with computer hardware. You should consult the installation guide that comes with your sound card hardware before you begin installing a new sound card.

 ⚡ WARNING   Opening your computer case could void your manufacturer's warranty. Be sure you check the documentation that came with your system before proceeding.

1   Turn off the power to your computer, disconnect all cables and power cords, and then open the case.

2   Locate a suitable interface slot inside the computer.

   Many newer systems have a mix of different types of interface slots, make sure you're using the appropriate slot for your interface card.

3   Install the sound card into an interface slot.

   The instruction guide that comes with the sound card will contain specific information about how to install the card into the interface slot.

4   Close the cover to your computer.

5   Connect your speakers to the sound card.

6   Plug in the power cord and other cables and turn the computer on.

Configuring a Sound Card

After you install the sound card in your computer, you must install the correct driver for it. With newer devices, Windows 95 can use the card's Plug and Play feature to detect the device and attempt to find and load the correct driver. With some older sound cards, you must manually configure them.

You can verify or change the settings of your sound card by using the Multimedia control panel.

Install the sound card driver

In this exercise, you configure the sound card on your system.

1   Click the Start menu, point to Settings, and then click Control Panel.

2   Double-click the Add New Hardware icon.

   The Add New Hardware Wizard starts.

3   Click Next in the next three windows.

   In the next three steps in the wizard, it detects your sound card, and then if necessary asks you to confirm your device.

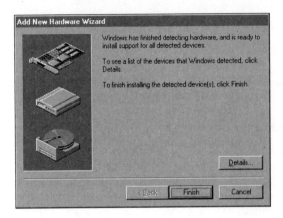

4 If necessary, select the new sound card, and then click OK, otherwise click finish.

After you confirm the sound card, Windows 95 installs the correct driver.

5 If you are prompted to restart Windows 95, click OK to restart your computer.

Configure the sound card

In most cases, the installed sound card begins working as soon as you have rebooted Windows 95. However, you might want to verify or adjust the settings of the sound card. In this exercise, you verify the configuration settings for the sound card.

1 Click the Start menu, point to Settings, and then click Control Panel.

2 Double-click the Multimedia icon.

3 Verify the settings on the Audio tab. The Preferred Device in the Playback and Recording areas should match your installed equipment. The Preferred Quality list box should show Radio Quality.

The higher the quality, the more memory and disk space are required to store the sounds. You can customize this option; however for most applications, the default of Radio Quality is more than adequate.

4 Click OK, and then close the Control Panel window.

Using the Media Player

You can use the Media Player to work with audio, video, and animation files. For example, you might have a video clip of a favorite artist singing and playing a song that you'd like to include in a presentation.

Because multimedia files are usually large, they are are stored on a compact disc, a local hard disk drive, a network file server, or another high-capacity storage medium. The playback quality is constrained by the amount of data that the storage medium can continuously supply to the file system. The faster the data can be read from the storage medium, the better the playback quality will be.

A multimedia file (such as an .AVI file) generally contains multiple components, such as digital-video data, audio data, text, and perhaps other data. As multimedia information is read, the multimedia hardware and software determines what the file contains, and then it separates and routes the data to the appropriate device.

The following table lists the types of files you can use with the Media Player.

Multimedia type	Filename extension
Animation	AVI
Digital-video	AVI
Musical Instrument Digital Interface (MIDI)	MID
Waveform-audio	WAV

Setting Up the Media Player

To use the Media Player, you must first install it. The Typical installation of Windows 95 does not include this program.

Install the Media Player

In this exercise, you install the Media Player component of Windows 95. If it is already installed, you can skip to the next exercise.

1 Click the Start menu, point to Settings, click Control Panel, and then double-click Add/Remove Programs.

2 Click the Windows Setup tab, scroll downward and click Multimedia, and then click Details.

3 Scroll through the list and verify that there is a checkmark in the check box next to Audio Compression, Media Player, Video Compression, and Volume Control.

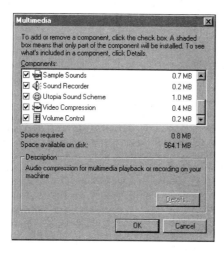

4   Click OK, and then click OK again.

5   If necessary, insert the Windows 95 disks or Windows 95 CD when you are prompted.

6   Click OK.

7   On the Control Panel window, click the Close button.

Playing a Multimedia File

Now that you've installed the drivers for the Media Player, you can play audio, video, and animation files.

Play a multimedia file

In this exercise you play the Skiing multimedia file. The Skiing file contains both sound and video.

1   Open the Start menu, point to Programs, point to Accessories, point to Multimedia, and then click Media Player.

2   On the File menu, click Open.

3   Click the Files Of Type down arrow, and then click Video For Windows (*.AVI).

4   In the More Windows SBS Practice folder, open the Exercises folder, and then double-click Skiing.

5   Click the Play button. After the multimedia file has finished playing, click the Close button on the Media Player window to close it.

Playing Waveform and MIDI Files

Windows 95 supports several types of sound files for recording and playback. The most common types of sound files are those recorded in the Microsoft Audio *waveform audio* format, or those recorded in the *Musical Instrument Digital Interface*, or *MIDI*, format.

Waveform audio files are similar to a tape recording of a sound. They are an analog audio signal, which can have a multitude of values at any given point, recorded as a digital file, which is composed merely of 0s and 1s. You can modify the speed and volume of a waveform audio file. You can also add special effects to a waveform audio file, such as echo or reverse. Waveform audio files are used for speech, messages, and other live recordings.

MIDI files are not a recording of a sound, but a set of instructions about what instruments are used to play the sound, what notes to play, and how fast to play them. MIDI files are often used for instrumental music, because the playback of the music uses the instruments as specified by the composer, rather than a recording of sounds made by an orchestra or band. MIDI is often used as a development tool for musicians. Virtually all advanced music equipment supports MIDI, and MIDI offers a convenient way to control the instrumentation very precisely.

You can think of the difference between waveform audio and MIDI files in this way. Suppose you want to make a recording of yourself singing "Happy Birthday" and you want to use a guitar as your accompaniment. You would use a waveform file to record your voice, because your voice continuously varies in pitch, volume, and timbre. You would use a MIDI file to create the accompaniment, using a guitar as the playback instrument, and specifying the notes and chords to play, because you can be certain that the right notes are played at the right time, using the right speed and instrument you want. Windows 95 comes with several wave and MIDI files stored in the C:\Windows\Media folder.

In the following exercises, you play a waveform audio file, and then you play a MIDI file.

Open the Media Player

If you don't see the Media Player or the Multimedia command, refer to the exercise "Setting up the Media Player."

1 Click the Start menu, point to Programs, point to Accessories, and then point to Multimedia.

2 Click Media Player.

The Media Player window opens.

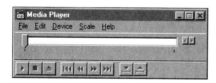

Play a waveform audio file

1 On the File menu, click Open.

By default, the Media Player opens the C:\Windows\Media folder and displays a list of files in the folder.

2 Click the Files Of Type down arrow, and then click Sound (*.wav).

3 Double-click the Chimes file.

4 Click the Play button.

The Chimes waveform audio file plays.

Play

5 In the taskbar, click the Speaker icon to display a shortcut menu and adjust the playback volume as needed.

If the sound file is short, you might not have time to adjust the playback volume before the file has finished playing.

Play a MIDI file

1 On the File menu, click Open.

2 Click the Files Of Type down arrow, and then click MIDI Sequencer (*.mid, *.rmi).

3 Double-click the Canyon file.

4 Click the Play button.

The Canyon MIDI file begins to play.

5 In the taskbar, click the Speaker icon to display a shortcut menu and adjust the playback volume as desired.

6 In the Media Player window, click the Stop button.

7 On the Media Player window, click the Close button.

Stop

Recording Sounds

Suppose you want to add a comment to your computer-based presentation. You want to give a little more explanation about your company to start off your first slide. You can create a sound file by using a microphone to record your comment.

You can record waveform audio files by using a microphone attached to your sound card, or you can record directly from an external source, such as a sound board mixer or a booster. Before you begin recording a sound, it's a good idea to check the Recording settings in the Multimedia Control Panel.

Verify the Recording settings

In this exercise you verify the Recording settings before you begin recording.

1 Click Start, point to Settings, point to Control Panel, and then double-click Multimedia.

2 Click the Audio tab.

3 Verify that the Volume slider in the Recording area is set to about the middle of the scale.

If on playback, your recording is faint or distorted, you can return to this dialog box to adjust the recording level.

4 Click OK.

Record your comments

In this exercise you record yourself commenting on your presentation.

NOTE If you do not have a microphone, you cannot record sounds in the following exercise. Skip to the next section, "Assigning Sounds to Events." to continue with the lesson.

1 Open the Start menu, point to Programs, point to Accessories, point to Multimedia, and then click Sound Recorder.

2 Position the microphone comfortably in front of you.

Record

Stop

3　Click the Record button.

4　Say "Childs Play, Inc. was founded by Henry Morgenstern to be the premier toy company of the Northwest." If you make a mistake, click New on the File menu to start over.

5　Click the Stop button.

 TIP You can add a dramatic flare to your recording by using the Echo command on the Effects menu. The addition of a slight echo can give your recording a "bigger" sound, much like what you might hear in an auditorium or concert hall. Use the commands on the Effects menu sparingly—they can quickly overwhelm your original recording. Echo, Speed, and Volume are all cumulative commands. For example, each time you click Increase Volume (by 25%) the recording will get progressively louder.

Play your new sound

Seek To Start

1　Click the Seek To Start button.

2　Click the Play button.

Save your new sound

1　On the File menu, click Save.

2　Verify that the path is set to C:\More Windows SBS Practice.

3　In the File Name box, type **Greetings to my customers** and then click OK.

4　On the Greetings To My Customers - Sound Recorder window, click the Close button.

Assigning Sounds to Events

An event is an action to which a program responds, such as pressing a key or clicking a button. For example, you might want to change the sound Windows 95 plays when you first start your computer, or you might want to change the sound that plays when you make an error.

Assign a sound to an event

In this exercise, you change the sound Windows 95 uses when you make an error.

1　Click Start, point to Settings, click Control Panel, and then double-click Sounds.

2　Scroll downward in the Events list, and click Default Sound.

3 Click Browse.

4 Click the Up One Level button twice, and then double-click the More Windows SBS Practice folder.

5 Select the waveform audio file named "UhOh."

6 Click OK, then click OK again.

7 On the Control Panel window, click the Close button.

8 On the Desktop, click Recycle Bin once to select it, and then press DELETE.

   Your new sound plays.

9 Close all open windows on your Desktop.

One Step Further: Embedding a Sound File into a Document

Earlier in this lesson, you saw how easy it is to create a sound file, now you'll embed a sound into a document. After you embed the sound file, you can play the file by opening the document and double-clicking the embedded file. You can use this technique to record a comment, for example, to the person who reviews your document.

Embed a sound file

In this exercise, you embed a sound file in a document.

1 From the More Windows SBS Practice folder, open the Exercises folder, and then open the Presentation Budget file.

2   On the Insert menu, click Object.

3   Click Create From File, and then click Browse.

       The Browse dialog box appears.

4   Make sure the Look In box displays More Windows SBS Practice.

5   Click Greetings To My Customers, and then click Insert.

6   Click OK.

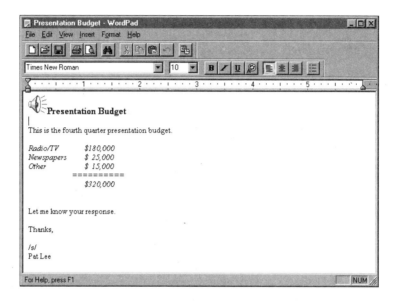

Play the sound file

1   Double-click the embedded object.

2   On the Budget Presentation - WordPad window, click the Save button.

3   On the WordPad window, click the Close button.

If you want to continue to the next lesson

➤ Close all open windows.

If you want to quit Windows 95 for now

1   Close all open windows.

2   On the Start menu, click Shut Down.

3   Click Shut Down The Computer, and then click Yes.

165

Lesson Summary

To	Do this	Button
Install a sound card	Turn off the power to your computer, open your computer, insert the sound card, close the computer, and then turn the computer on.	
Install a sound card driver	Open the Start menu, point to Settings, open Control Panel, and then open Add Hardware. Click Next three times. Select the device and click OK. Click OK again.	
Configure a sound card	Open the Start menu, point to Settings, open Control Panel, and then open Multimedia. Verify or adjust the settings for audio or MIDI files. Click OK.	
Install the Media Player	Open the Start menu, point to Settings, click the Control Panel, and then open Add/Remove Programs. Click the Windows Setup tab, click Multimedia, and then click Details. Scroll through the list and place a checkmark in the check boxes for Audio Compression, Media Player, Video Compression, and Volume Control. Click OK three time to return to the Control Panel window, and then close the window.	
Play a multimedia file	Open the Start menu, point to Programs, point to Accessories, point to Multimedia, and then click Media Player. On the File menu, click Open. Click the Files Of Type down arrow and select Video for Windows (*.avi). Open the folder that contains the multimedia file. Open the multimedia file.	
Play a waveform audio file	Open the Start menu, point to Programs, point to Accessories, point to Multimedia, and then click Media Player. On the File menu, click Open. Click the Files Of Type down arrow, and then click Sound (*.wav). Open a waveform audio file. Click the Play button.	▶

To	Do this	Button
Play a MIDI file	Open the Start menu, point to Programs, point to Accessories, point to Multimedia, and then click Media Player. On the File menu, click Open. Click the Files Of Type down arrow, and then click MIDI Sequencer (*.mid, *.rmi). Open a MIDI file. Click the Play button.	
Record a waveform audio file	Open the Start menu, point to Programs, point to Accessories, point to Multimedia, and then click Sound Recorder. Click the Record button. Record your speech using the microphone. Click the Stop button.	
Play the recorded sound	Click the Seek To Start button. Click the Play button.	
Save the recorded sound	On the File menu, click Save. Verify that the path is set to the folder where you want to save the file. In the File Name box, type a filename. Click OK.	
Assign a sound to a Windows 95 event	Open the Start menu, point to Settings, click the Control Panel, and then open Sounds. Scroll downward in the Events list and click an event. Click Browse. Scroll through the selection of waveform audio files in the Media folder. Click OK, then click OK again. On the Control Panel window, click the Close button.	

For online information about	From the Help dialog box, click Index and then type
Installing a sound card	**sound cards, setting up device cards**
Configuring a sound card	**configuring, multimedia devices**
Installing the Media Player	**multimedia, installing multimedia devices**
Playing a multimedia file	**playing, multimedia files**
Playing a sound file	**playing, sound files**
Recording a waveform audio file	**recording sound files**
Assigning a sound to a Windows 95 event	**events, assigning sound to**

Preview of the Next Lesson

In the next lesson, you'll learn to work with your CD-ROM drive to play music discs. You'll modify the disc information for the artist, the disc title, and then the track information. You'll also modify the play list so that you can hear the songs you want in the order you want to hear them.

Using Your CD-ROM Drive with Music Discs

In this lesson you will learn how to:

Estimated time
40 min.

- Set up a CD-ROM drive.
- Play audio CDs on your CD-ROM drive.
- Make copies of audio tracks.

With Windows 95, it's easy to use your CD-ROM drive to play music. You can play any music CD, modify the name of the CD and its music tracks, and set up a custom play list. You can also use your CD-ROM drive to install new software that you purchase. Installing software from a CD-ROM disc is much easier than installing from several floppy disks, and the CD-ROM might provide additional files, such as multimedia games that are too large to fit on a floppy disk.

Setting Up a CD-ROM Drive

Many computers purchased today come with a CD-ROM drive installed. However, you might have an older computer that you're upgrading to work with Windows 95, and you might want to install a CD-ROM player. After you install the hardware for the CD-ROM drive, you need to install the CD-ROM drivers—the software needed to run the CD-ROM drive.

The first step in using a CD-ROM drive is setting it up. Assuming that you've purchased a new CD-ROM drive, you can use the Add New Hardware feature in Control Panel to install the necessary drivers.

Suppose, for example, that you've just purchased new integrated sound and CD-ROM hardware that you want to use in your computer. The CD-ROM hardware includes the interface card and the CD-ROM drive itself. Your CD-ROM might also include a set of speakers and possibly a microphone. If it does, you probably have a card that combines sound support and the CD-ROM interface in one adapter card. The installation process for either a CD-ROM only or a combined sound and CD-ROM interface card is basically the same. If you have a combined card, you'll also have the added step of configuring your sound card too. (See Lesson 8 for more information about installing and configuring a sound card.)

You want to install the new hardware, and then set it up for use with Windows 95. Because you didn't have the CD-ROM hardware installed when you installed Windows 95, you'll also want to install the CD Player software component so you can play audio CDs.

In the next exercises, you install the CD-ROM drive and drivers, and then you install the CD Player. This exercise assumes that you are installing an internal CD-ROM drive into your computer. Consult the installation guide that came with your CD-ROM drive for more information on how to install the CD-ROM drive.

 WARNING The internal components of your computer are very sensitive to static electricity. If you are not experienced with installing computer devices, it is recommended that you have a qualified service professional install the CD-ROM drive for you.

Install the CD-ROM hardware

This exercise is a brief overview that describes how to install a CD-ROM drive. Some of the steps involve more detail than can be discussed in this book, and they assume that you have some familiarity with computer hardware. You should consult the installation guide that comes with your CD-ROM hardware before you begin installing a new CD-ROM drive.

 WARNING Opening your computer case could void your manufacturer's warranty. Be sure you check the documentation that came with your system before proceeding.

1   Turn off the power to your computer, disconnect all cables and power cords, and then open the case.

2   Insert the CD-ROM card into an available expansion slot.

 WARNING Whenever you install a card into an expansion slot, never force the card into the slot. If it doesn't quite fit, try using another expansion slot.

3   Install the CD-ROM drive, connecting the computer power supply cable to the
    drive power receptacle, and the CD-ROM data line to the CD-ROM card.

    Depending on the type of data cable you are using, you might need to verify that
    the colored edge of the data cable aligns with pin 1 of the CD-ROM drive and the
    interface card.

4   Connect the speakers to the sound device card, and the power supply to the
    speakers.

    Many speaker sets that are manufactured explicitly for computer multimedia will
    be self-amplified speakers and will need to be plugged into a power outlet. Typi-
    cally, you can't use a power supply cable from inside your computer for this
    purpose. You will need to use a standard wall outlet.

5   Close the cover to your computer, connect the cables and power cords, and turn
    your computer on.

 TIP   If your CD-ROM interface card is not Plug and Play compatible, you
might want to keep the cover to your computer off until you have verified that
the interface card is working properly and there are no conflicts with other
devices.

Install the CD-ROM driver

1   Open the Start menu, point to Settings, click Control Panel, and then open Add
    New Hardware.

2   Click Next, and then click Next again.

3   After a few moments, Windows 95 will locate the CD-ROM card, and ask you to
    confirm the type of CD-ROM drive you have.

    If your CD-ROM is not detected, it is recommended that you obtain an updated
    device driver that is compatible with Windows 95. You should still be able to
    install your device driver from an MS-DOS prompt using the installation software
    provided by the manufacturer; however, some Windows 95 features might not be
    functional until you have updated the driver.

4   Select the CD-ROM drive, and then click Install.

5   Click OK three times to restart Windows 95.

Install the CD Player

1   Click Start, point to Settings, point to Control Panel, and then double-click Add
    New Programs.

2   Click the Windows Setup tab.

3   Click Multimedia and then click Details.

4 Click the check box next to CD Player to select it.

5 Click OK.

Windows 95 begins installing the CD Player. If prompted, insert the Windows 95 installation disks.

6 On the Control Panel window, click the Close button.

Playing a Music Disc

After you've installed the CD-ROM drive and its driver, you can play a music CD. To play a music CD, you insert the CD into the CD-ROM drive. The AutoPlay feature of Windows 95 detects that you have inserted an audio CD into your CD-ROM drive and then starts the CD Player. If the device driver for your CD-ROM drive is not Windows 95 compatible, it will not support AutoPlay. You can still use the CD Player to play a music CD. (You can contact the manufacturer of your CD-ROM for Windows 95 compatible device drivers.)

AutoPlay makes it very easy to play audio CDs. You just insert the audio CD into the drive and sit back and enjoy. With AutoPlay, you don't need to worry about the exact commands to play the CD.

 NOTE To manually play an Audio CD, click Start, point to Programs, point to Accessories, point to Multimedia, and then click CD Player. Then click the Play button.

Play a music CD

1 Open the CD-ROM drive door.

2 Insert any music CD-ROM.

Some older CD-ROM drives use special cases, called caddies, to hold the disc while it was inserted into the drive. Depending on the type of drive you have you might need to use a caddy.

If your CD has a powered drive door, don't force the drive door closed manually. Use the open/close button.

3 Close the CD-ROM drive door.

The CD Player starts and the CD begins playing.

 TIP You can turn off AutoPlay just for the CD you're inserting by holding down SHIFT when you insert the CD into the CD-ROM drive. To disable or enable the AutoPlay feature for this and subsequent CDs, open any folder and, on the View menu, click Option. Click File Types In the Registered File Types list box, click AudioCD, and then click Edit. In the Action list box, click Play and then click Set Default to toggle the AutoPlay feature off or on. Close the Options dialog box.

View the CD Player settings

In this exercise, you become familiar with the settings in the CD Player window.

1 Click the CD Player button on the taskbar.

The CD Player window opens.

2 On the View menu, click Toolbar and then click Toolbar again.

The Toolbar toggles off and on.

3 On the View menu, click Disk/Track Info, and then click Disk/Track Info to toggle it on.

4 On the View menu, click Status Bar, and then click Status Bar again to toggle it on.

The Status Bar appears.

Skip tracks (songs)

Next Track

1 In the CD Player window, click the Next Track button.

The next track begins playing.

2 In the CD Player window, click the Previous Track button.

The previous track begins playing.

Previous Track

Pause and restart playback of an audio CD

Pause

1 In the CD Player window, click the Pause button.

2 In the CD Player window, click the Play button.

Start WordPad while playing an audio CD

Play

Now that you've got your CD playing, you need to get back to work. You don't need to wait for your CD to finish playing before going on to your next task. With Windows 95, you can run CD Player and continue to work on your presentation—simultaneously.

1 With the music still playing, click the Start button. Point to Programs, point to Accessories, and then click WordPad.

173

2   Type **This is a test of multitasking**.

3   On the File menu, click Save As, and save your file with the name **Mtest.wri**

4   On the WordPad window, click the Close button.

WordPad closes and the CD continues to play.

Editing a Music Play List

By default, the CD play list (a list of songs on an audio CD) contains no information about the CD other than the number of tracks and their length. You can modify the play list to add the artist's name, the title of the CD, and the name of each track (song) of music. By using a play list, you can keep track of which song is playing. You can also modify the order of the songs on the play list. After you create a play list for a specific CD, Windows 95 will remember it and use it automatically every time you play the CD.

For example, you might have a favorite CD that you like to play, but there are a few songs you don't care to hear. And there's one track you'd like to listen to several times. You can modify the play list to skip the songs you don't like, add the same track several times to repeat the songs you do like, or change the order in which the songs are played.

 NOTE   The contents of the CD Player Play List are stored in the \Windows\Cdplayer.ini file. You can modify its contents using WordPad, NotePad, or any program that can edit text files.

In the next exercises, you modify the play list.

Modify the Contents of the Available Tracks

Edit Play List

1   In the CD Player window, click the Edit Play List button.

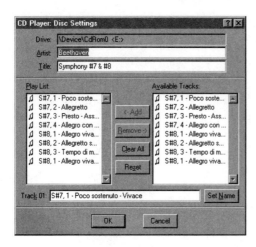

2   Select the text in the Artist box, and type the name of the artist.

3   Select the text in the Title box, and type the title of the CD.

4   Select the text for Track 01 in the Available Tracks list, type the title of the first song, and press **ENTER**.

   You can usually get the list of songs on a CD from the CD's case.

5   Keep typing the titles for each track and press **ENTER** until all the tracks are named.

6   Click OK.

Modify the play list sequence

1   In the CD Player window, click the Edit Play List button, and then click the Clear All button.

   All the entries, if any, are cleared from the Play List area in the Disk Settings dialog box.

2   In the CD Player window, click a track title and click Add.

   The track is added to the play list.

To add all the titles in one step, you can select all the titles and then click Add.

3   Continue clicking a track title and the Add button until all the tracks you want to play are selected.

4   Click OK.

5   Click the Play button.

   The tracks begin playing in the order you specified.

Set the Preferences for the CD Player

You might want to have the CD Player play the same CD continuously, or you might want to hear the songs on the CD but in random order. You can change the options for the CD Player so that you can listen to the music continually or in random order.

Set the random play option

In this exercise, you modify the options to play the tracks in random order. Then you modify the options to repeat the tracks in the play list.

Random Track Order

Play

1   Click the Random Track Order button.

2   Click the Play button.

   The CD begins playing the tracks in random order.

3   Click the down arrow next to the Track text box.

   The play list appears in random order.

Next Track

4 Click the down arrow again and click the Next Track button.

A different track begins playing.

5 Click the Stop button.

6 Click the Random Track Order button again.

This resets the CD Player to its original status.

Stop

Random Track Order

Set the continuous play option

1 Click the Continuous Play button.

2 Click the Play button.

The CD begins playing the tracks.

Continuous Play

3 When you have finished listening to the music CD, click the Stop button.

The CD stops playing.

Play

4 On the CD Player window, click the Close button.

5 Remove the CD from the CD-ROM drive.

One Step Further: Creating a Shortcut to an Audio CD or a Music Track

If you do not have a Windows 95 compatible device driver for your CD-ROM drive, you will not be able to do this exercise. Go on to the next lesson.

You can create a shortcut to an audio CD, which creates a link to a specific track on any audio CD, such as track 01. You can also copy a track, which creates a link to a specific CD.

1 In the My Computer window, use the right mouse button to click the icon for your CD-ROM drive.

2 On the shortcut menu, click Open, click Track01 once to select it and then click Copy on the Edit menu.

3 Use the right mouse button to click the Desktop, and then on the shortcut menu, click Paste Shortcut.

You now have a shortcut to track 01 on your Desktop for any CD that you put in your CD-ROM drive. If you want, you can place this shortcut in your StartUp folder. Then, the first track of any audio CD that you have in your CD-ROM drive will start playing each time you start your computer.

4 From the CD-ROM window, drag the icon for Track03 to the Desktop, and place it next to the shortcut for Track01.

You now have a copy of Track03 on your Desktop for the specific CD that is in the CD-ROM drive. If you want, you can place this copy of Track03 in your StartUp folder. Then, the third track in the play list for this CD will begin playing each time you start your computer. If this specific CD is not in the CD-ROM drive when you start up your computer, you will be notified with a message box.

5   Remove the audio CD, and then double-click the Track03 icon.

A message indicates that the correct CD is not in the CD-ROM drive.

6   Click OK to close the message box, and then close the CD Player window.

7   Hold down the SHIFT key and insert another audio CD in the CD-ROM.

8   Double-click the shortcut icon for Track01.

The audio CD starts at track 1.

If you want to continue to the next lesson

➤   Close all open windows.

If you want to quit Windows 95 for now

1   Close all open windows.

2   On the Start menu, click Shut Down.

3   Select Shut Down The Computer, and then click Yes.

Lesson Summary

To	Do this	Button
Install the CD-ROM hardware	Turn off the power to the computer. Remove the cover of the computer. Install the CD-ROM drive and the CD-ROM card following the instructions on the installation guide that came with your CD-ROM drive. Connect the power supply and the data lines. Connect the speakers to the CD-ROM card. Close the cover to the computer and turn it on.	
Install a CD-ROM driver	Open the Start menu, point to Settings, click Control Panel, and open Add New Hardware. Click Next twice, and then select the CD-ROM card. Click Install. Click OK twice, and then click OK to restart Windows 95.	
Play a music disc	Insert the disc in the CD-ROM drive.	
Skip tracks	In the CD Player window, click the Previous Track or Next Track button.	◀◀ ▶▶
Pause the CD Player	In the CD Player window, click the Pause button.	❚❚

To	Do this	Button
Restart the CD Player	In the CD Player window, click the Play button.	▶
Modify the descriptions of the available tracks	In the CD Player window, click the Edit Play List button. Type the artist's name and the title. Type the names for each track and pressing ENTER until all the tracks are named. Click OK.	
Modify the Play List sequence	In the CD Player window, click the Clear All button. In the CD Player window, click a track title and click Add. Continue clicking track titles and then the Add button until all the tracks you want to play are selected. Click OK, and then click Play.	
Set the random play option	In the CD Player window, click the Random Track Order button.	
Set the continuous play option	In the CD Player window, click the Continuous Play button.	

For online information about	From the CD Player Help dialog box, click Index and then type
Playing a music disc	**Playing CDs**, then choose **Playing a CD**
Editing a music play list	**play list**, then choose **Specifying which tracks to play and in which order**
Play the tracks on a CD in random order	**random order, playing tracks in**

Preview of the Next Lessons

In Part 4, "Working with Microsoft Plus!" you'll learn how to enhance your system and networking capabilities with Microsoft Plus! In the next lesson, you'll install Microsoft Plus! and use its features to improve the appearance and functionality of Windows 95.

Review & Practice

In the lessons in Part 3, "Using Multimedia," you learned how to work with multimedia files and how to use your CD-ROM drive to play music discs. If you want to practice these skills and test your understanding before you proceed with the lessons in Part 4, you can work through the Review & Practice section following this lesson.

Review & Practice

Estimated time
20 min.

You will review and practice how to:

- Record and play sound files.
- Play a music CD and edit a play list.

Before you go on to Part 4, you can practice the skills you learned in Part 3 by working through the steps in this Review & Practice section.

Scenario

You have successfully set up the computers in your home office. Because of your experience with Windows 95, you've been asked to help your corporate office co-workers set up their computers to record and play sound files. You've also volunteered to demonstrate how to play music CDs and edit the play list.

Step 1: Record and Play Sound Files

In this step, you'll record a new sound file. You'll embed this sound file into a WordPad document, and then you'll play the sound file.

Record a sound file

1   Open the Sound Recorder program.

2   Record the following comment: "Sales projections are up 25% over last year."

3   Add an echo effect to your sound file.

179

   4   Save your file to the Desktop with the name **Sales Projections**

Play a sound file

   1   Open the Media Player.
   2   Open the Sales Projections file.
   3   Play the sound file.
   4   Close the Sales Projections - Sound Recorder window.

Step 2:   Play a Music CD and Edit the Play List

   ➤   Insert a music CD into the CD-ROM drive. (Hint: If your CD-ROM drive doesn't support AutoPlay, click Start, point to Programs, point to Accessories, point to Multimedia and then click CD Player.)

Edit the play list

   1   Click the Edit Play List button on the CD Player window.
   2   Enter in the name of the artist, title of the CD and the title of each track (song).
   3   Edit the Play List so that the first track plays between all the other tracks. (Hint: The play list sequence would show Track01, Track02, Track01, Track03, Track01, Track04 and so on.)
   4   When you have finished listening to the CD, close the CD Player window.

For more information on	See
Playing multimedia files	**Lesson 8**
Recording waveform files	**Lesson 8**
Playing Audio CDs	**Lesson 9**
Edit an Audio CDs play list	**Lesson 9**

Finish the Review & Practice

   1   Close all open windows.
   2   If any window is minimized, use the right mouse button to click the window's taskbar button, and then click Close.

   You are now ready to start the next lesson, or you can work on your own.

   3   If you are finished using Windows 95 for now, on the Start menu click Shut Down, then click Yes.

Working with Microsoft Plus!

Enhancing Your System with Microsoft Plus!

In this lesson you will learn how to:

- Install Microsoft Plus!
- Use Desktop themes to modify the appearance of Windows 95.
- Use full window drag and font smoothing.
- Work with the System Agent to schedule system maintenance tasks.
- Use DriveSpace 3 for maximum disk compression.

In this lesson you'll learn to work with Microsoft Plus!, a companion product for Windows 95 that takes advantage of the processing power available from Intel 486 and Pentium computers and can enhance your work with Windows 95. You'll need to have at least a 486 computer to successfully use Microsoft Plus!

In this lesson, you'll install Microsoft Plus!, and then you'll use Desktop themes to enhance the appearance of Windows 95. You'll change the background of your Desktop, all of the standard icons, and the screen saver to match a common theme. You'll use full window drag and font smoothing to make it easier to work with the Windows 95 interface. You'll schedule routine computer maintenance programs to run automatically with the System Agent, and you'll use DriveSpace 3 to get more data on your disks.

NOTE You'll need to have Microsoft Plus!, which is purchased separately from Windows 95, to complete the exercises in this lesson and in Lesson 11 of this book.

Installing Microsoft Plus!

Suppose you have a high-powered computer, such as a system with a Pentium processor, a Super VGA screen supporting high color or true color, a large hard disk, and fast access to the Internet. Windows 95 works very well with such a powerful computer; but you would probably like to use your computer to its fullest capabilities. Microsoft Plus! is a set of enhancements to Windows 95 that can make it easier and more enjoyable to get your work done on a 486 or Pentium computer. Microsoft Plus! has several features that work specifically with the resources available on fast, powerful computers.

Microsoft Plus! includes the following components.

System Agent schedules system maintenance programs to start and stop at specific times under the circumstances that you specify.

DriveSpace 3 compresses the most data possible onto your disks.

Desktop Themes modifies the appearance of the Desktop, and makes it easier and more enjoyable for you to work in the Windows 95 environment.

Network and Internet Additions makes working with remote computers easier to set up and to use.

Installing Microsoft Plus! is easy. You insert the Microsoft Plus! CD into your computer's CD-ROM drive. The Windows 95 AutoPlay feature starts the Microsoft Plus! Setup program. When the setup screen appears, you choose the options you want and install Microsoft Plus!

TIP If your CD-ROM drive doesn't support AutoPlay, you can install Microsoft Plus! by double-clicking the Autorun icon or Setup icon in the Microsoft Plus! folder.

Install Microsoft Plus!

In this exercise, you install Microsoft Plus!

AutoPlay, normally associated with audio compact discs, also works with data discs if there is an Autorun.inf file on the disc.

1   Insert the Microsoft Plus! CD into your CD-ROM drive.

The AutoPlay feature of Windows 95 senses that the CD is inserted, and the Autorun program starts. The Microsoft Plus! For Windows 95 window appears.

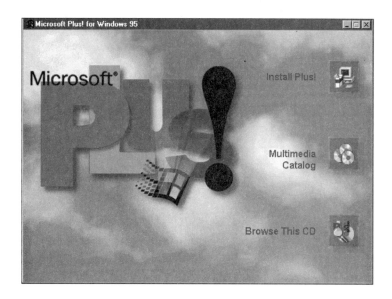

2 Click the Install Plus! icon.

After a few moments, the Microsoft Plus! For Windows 95 Setup window appears, with the Microsoft Plus! For Windows 95 Setup dialog box on top.

3 After reading the license agreement, click Continue.

The Name and Organization Information window appears.

4 In the Name box, type your name; then, in the Organization box, type the name of your organization.

5 Click OK.

The Confirm Name And Organization Information window appears.

6 Click OK.

The Microsoft Plus! For Windows 95 Setup window appears for you to type your CD key.

7 Locate the CD key (on the sticker of the CD liner notes or CD sleeve), and in the CD Key box, type your CD key.

The Microsoft Plus! For Windows 95 Setup window appears for you to confirm your CD key.

8 Click OK.

The Microsoft Plus! For Windows 95 Setup window appears for you to confirm the installation location.

Choose the location for the installation

1   Verify that the folder is C:\Program Files\Plus!

You can click the Change Folder button if you want to install Microsoft Plus! to another location.

2   Click OK.

The Setup program begins searching for any installed components. After a few moments, the Microsoft Plus! For Windows 95 Setup window appears.

If you want to choose the Custom installation, click the Custom button.

3   Click the Typical button.

The Run System-Maintenance Tasks At Night dialog box appears.

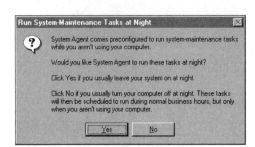

Choose the System Agent options

In this exercise, you determine how you want System Agent to schedule maintenance tasks. System Agent automatically schedules ScanDisk and Defragmenter to run when you are least likely to need your computer. If you leave your computer on overnight, you'll probably want to have your computer maintenance tasks done during the night. If you turn your computer off at the end of the day, however, you'll probably want System Agent to pick likely times and conditions during the day to run the maintenance programs when your computer is idle.

    Click Yes if you want to run maintenance tasks at night; click No if you want to run maintenance tasks during your normal business hours.

The Setup program continues the installation.

Continue with the installation

1   If you do not have a sound card, the Sound Check window appears in which you can verify whether you want to install the sound files anyway. To install the sound files, click Yes; otherwise, click No.

The Setup program continues the installation. After a few moments, the Win95 Installation window appears.

2   Click OK.

3 If the Copying Files window appears, insert the Microsoft Windows 95 CD into the CD-ROM drive, and then click OK.

IMPORTANT   If you're installing the Internet components of Microsoft Plus! there are required network files that must be copied from the Windows 95 installation CD. The network files come with Windows 95 because many other programs might need to use them.

Setup continues the installation. After a few moments, the Internet Setup Wizard appears.

Install the Internet components

1 Click Next.

The Internet Setup Wizard window appears for you to choose how to connect to the Internet.

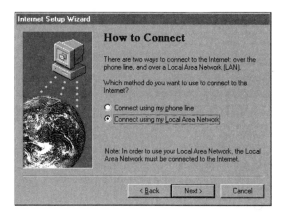

2   Click Connect Using My Phone Line, and click Next.

If you connect through your Local Area Network, click Connect Using My Local Area Network. The Internet Setup Wizard window appears.

3   Click The Microsoft Network option, and then click Next.

If you access the Internet through your local provider, click the I Already Have An Account With A Different Service Provider option.

The Internet Setup Wizard window appears for you to confirm the installation of the files.

4   Click Next.

The Copying Files window appears. After a few moments, the Internet Setup Wizard window appears for you to confirm that you are a member of The Microsoft Network.

 IMPORTANT   You must be a member of The Microsoft Network to use it as an Internet access provider.

---

5   Click Yes.

If you click No, then you'll be presented with a series of windows to enter your name, personal information, and billing information. See Lesson 5, "Connecting to The Microsoft Network," for more details.

6   Click Next.

The Microsoft Network window appears.

7   Click OK.

The Microsoft Network window appears for you to enter the first three digits of your phone number.

8   Verify that the area code in the Your Area Or City Code box is correct; then, type the first three digits of your phone number in the next text box and click OK.

The Microsoft Network window appears for you to confirm that the Setup program will get the latest Internet access phone numbers from The Microsoft Network.

9   Click Connect.

The Sign In window appears.

10   In the Member ID box, type your member ID. In the Password box, type your password, and then click Connect.

The sign in program uses your modem to connect to The Microsoft Network and download the latest access phone numbers for The Microsoft Network. After a few moments, the new phone numbers are downloaded. The Microsoft Network window appears for you to confirm the new number.

11   Click OK.

The Internet Setup Wizard window appears.

12   Click OK.

The Building Driver Information Database window appears. After a few moments, the Copying Files window appears as the setup program installs the files. After a few more moments, the Set Up A Desktop Theme window appears.

13   Click OK.

14   Click Cancel.

You'll select a Desktop theme in the next section. The Microsoft Plus! For Windows 95 - Restart Windows window appears. You must restart Windows 95 for all the components in Microsoft Plus! to become active.

Restart Windows 95

1   Click Restart Windows.

After a few moments, Windows 95 restarts.

2   Log back onto Windows 95.

The Desktop reappears. The icon for the System Agent appears on the Taskbar next to the Clock.

The Internet
Explorer

System Agent

Modifying the Appearance of Windows 95

You can change many of the aesthetic aspects of Windows 95 by using several features of Microsoft Plus! You can use Desktop themes to alter the appearance of icons and the background, and add screen savers, mouse pointers, and so on. You can enable full window dragging and font smoothing to make it easier work in Windows 95.

Setting Desktop Themes

Desktop themes are a collection of settings that affect the way your Desktop looks and works. A Desktop theme includes a background wallpaper, a screen saver, a color scheme, and a set of sounds, cursors, icons, and fonts. You can use the theme as it is, or you can change any of its components. You can mix and match between themes.

There are two classes of Desktop themes. One class is designed for monitors that support 256 colors. The other is for monitors that support high color (65,535 colors) or better. You can use either type of Desktop theme on a monitor that supports 256 colors; however, some of the Desktop theme features might not appear clearly if your monitor doesn't support high color.

In the next exercises, you select various Desktop themes. Then, you preview how the new look will appear on your Desktop. Finally, you apply the Desktop theme to the Desktop.

Select a Desktop theme

1 Click Start, point to Settings, and click Control Panel.

2 In the Control Panel window, double-click Desktop Themes.

Desktop Themes

The Desktop Themes window opens. The preview area displays a sample Desktop showing your current color scheme, fonts, wallpaper, and so on.

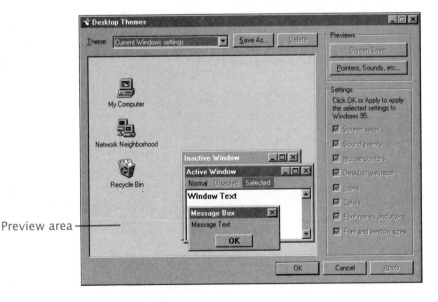

Preview area

3 Click the Themes down arrow and click Dangerous Creatures (256 color).

The Multiple File Import Filter window appears while the theme file is opened, and then the preview window displays a sample Desktop showing how the Dangerous Creatures theme will modify it.

4 Click the Themes down arrow and click Travel (high color).

The preview window displays a sample Desktop showing the new theme.

Preview the screen saver changes

Each theme has a corresponding screen saver, which you can preview prior to applying it to your Desktop.

1 Click the Screen Saver button.

After a moment the screen saver starts.

2 Move the mouse or press the SPACEBAR to stop the screen saver.

Preview the pointer, sounds, and other changes

Corresponding mouse pointers, sounds, and Desktop icons are available as part of each theme.

1 Click the Themes down arrow, click Windows 95 (256 color), and then click the Pointers, Sounds, Etc. button.

The Preview Windows 95 (256 color) window appears.

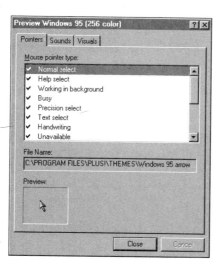

2   In the Mouse Pointer Type list, click Busy.

A preview of the Busy pointer appears in the Preview area of the dialog box. The preview shows how the mouse pointer will appear when Windows 95 is busy processing and is not able to accept input from you.

3   Click the Sounds tab to display a list of sounds associated with Windows 95 events.

4   In the Sound Event list, click Default Sound, and then click the Play button.

The default sound plays. The default sound is the sound that plays when an event doesn't match any of the other events in the Sound Event list.

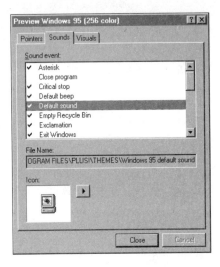

5   Click the Visuals tab to display a list of pictures associated with Windows 95 items.

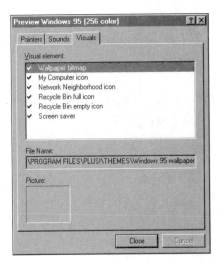

6   In the Visual Element list, click Recycle Bin Full Icon.

The Picture area previews the icon that will appear on your Desktop when Recycle Bin has folders or files in it.

7   Click Close.

Apply the Desktop theme

1   Click the Apply button.

The Windows 95 theme is applied to the Desktop. Your screen should look like this.

New Desktop Theme

2   On the Control Panel window, click the Close button.

The Control Panel window closes.

Modifying a Desktop Theme

After you have selected a Desktop theme, you can modify it by changing selected elements using the Control Panel icons. For example, you can change the background wallpaper or mouse pointer.

Change the font for the title bar

In this exercise, you modify the Desktop theme by changing the font used in a window's title.

1   Use the right mouse button to click the Desktop, and then click Properties.

The Properties window appears.

2   Click the Appearance tab.

The settings for the Desktop appearance appear.

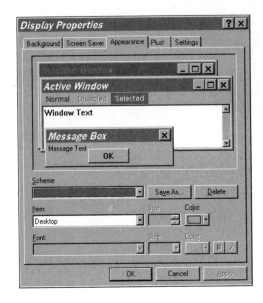

Bold

Italic

3   Click the Item down arrow, and then click Active Title Bar.

You can also click the Active Window title bar in the preview window.

4   Click the Font down arrow, and then click Comic Sans MS or any font you prefer.

5   Click the Bold and Italic buttons to deselect bold and italic.

6   Click OK to change the font for all window title bars.

Using Full Window Drag and Font Smoothing

Two of the enhancements for Microsoft Plus!, full window drag and font smoothing, are more subtle than Desktop themes, yet they play a part in making the screen appearance more attractive.

If full window drag is enabled, when you drag an opened window on the Desktop, you see the full window rather than just the outline. Full window drag makes Windows 95 take more time to redraw an image as it is dragged; so if speed is a concern, you might want to turn this feature off. (Any time an element on your screen changes, such as when you move a window, Windows 95 has to redraw all of the portions of the screen that are affected. When you use full window drag, Windows 95 has more information to redraw.) If font smoothing is enabled, fonts displayed at a large size on your screen appear without the stairstep effect called *jaggies*. Font smoothing (also called anti-aliasing) requires a monitor and video display that can support 16-bit color (High Color), 24-bit color (True Color), or greater.

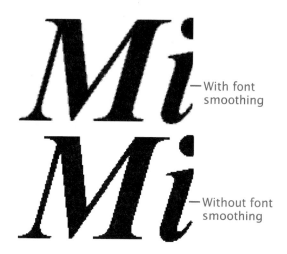

—With font smoothing

—Without font smoothing

In the next exercises, you examine full window drag and font smoothing.

Examine full window drag

1   On the Desktop, double-click the My Computer icon.

2   Make sure the window is not maximized, and drag the window up and down a few times.

The contents appear in the window as it is being dragged.

Examine font smoothing

NOTE   If you do not have a video display that supports High Color or True Color, go on to the next exercise.

1   In the My Computer window, double-click the Drive C icon, and then double-click the More Windows SBS Practice folder.

2   In the More Windows SBS Practice folder window, double-click the Exercise folder and then double-click the Microsoft Plus! file.

The file opens, displaying a message in a large font.

3 Click the Maximize button.

The file fills the Desktop.

4 After viewing the file, click the Restore button.

By default, full window drag and font smoothing are enabled when you install Microsoft Plus! You can turn these features off or on using the Display Properties window. When you install Microsoft Plus!, a new tab for Microsoft Plus! settings is added to the Display Properties window.

Change the settings for full window drag and font smoothing

In this exercise, you open the Display Properties window to change the settings for full windows drag and font smoothing.

1 Use the right mouse button to click the Desktop, and then click Properties.

The Display Properties window appears.

2 Click the Plus! tab.

The display settings for Microsoft Plus! appear.

3 Click the check box next to Show Window Contents While Dragging to remove the checkmark.

Removing this checkmark disables the full window drag feature.

4 Click the check box next to Smooth Edges Of Screen Fonts to remove the checkmark.

Removing this checkmark disables the font smoothing feature. If you do not have a video display that supports High Color or True Color, you can skip this step.

5 Click the OK button on the Display Properties window.

If you have Microsoft Word installed on your computer, you'll probably see the file open in that program instead of in WordPad.

6 Scan the WordPad - Microsoft Plus! window.

Notice that the fonts are more jagged.

If your video display does not support High Color or True Color, you won't see any difference.

7 Drag the WordPad - Microsoft Plus! window up and down.

The outline of the window moves, not the window.

8 Click the Close button on the WordPad - Microsoft Plus! window.

If you see a dialog box asking if you want to save changes, click No.

Restore the Microsoft Plus! settings

1 Use the right mouse button to click the Desktop, and then click Properties.

2 Click the Plus! tab.

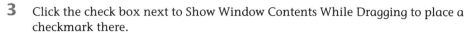

3   Click the check box next to Show Window Contents While Dragging to place a checkmark there.

Placing this checkmark enables the full window drag feature.

4   Click the check box next to Smooth Edges Of Screen Fonts to place a checkmark there.

Placing this checkmark enables the font smoothing feature.

5   Click the OK button on the Display Properties window.

6   Hold down SHIFT, and then click the Close button on the More Windows SBS Practice window.

Working with the System Agent

System Agent is a tool that you can use to monitor your system and perform several maintenance tasks while you are doing other tasks. System Agent starts actions at the times and under conditions that you specify. Suppose you find that you want to run ScanDisk (a program that checks your disk for errors) every morning at 10:30, or you want to run Disk Defragmenter (a program that groups file clusters contiguously for efficient reading and writing of your files) every Friday evening. Of course, you can run these tasks manually at any time, but you can use System Agent to perform these tasks for you—automatically at specified intervals, days, and times and under the conditions that you specify. (For more information about Disk Defragmenter and ScanDisk, see Lesson 3,"Managing Your Hard Disk.")

By default, System Agent is set up to run disk maintenance related tasks when you are likely to be away from your computer. For example, most users are asleep from 10 p.m. to 6 a.m., so System Agent schedules the Disk Defragmenter for 12:00 midnight. If your computer is not running at the time System Agent has scheduled a task to run, the next time you start your computer, System Agent will display a message box and inform you of the missed schedule. You can then reschedule the task if you want.

Setting Up a Task

After you install Microsoft Plus!, System Agent is set up to start whenever you start your computer, and its icon appears in the Taskbar. To modify the settings in System Agent, you can use the System Agent icon to open the System Agent window. Then you can add, modify, or delete tasks (programs).

Set up a task

In this exercise you set up a task in System Agent.

System Agent

1   With the right mouse button, click the System Agent icon on the Taskbar, and then click Open.

The System Agent window opens showing the schedules for each task.

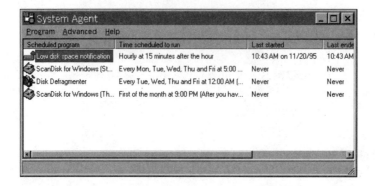

2   On the Program menu, click Schedule A New Program.

     The Schedule A New Program window appears.

3   Click the Program down arrow and click ScanDisk for Windows.

     ScanDisk for Windows is selected.

4   Click the When To Run button.

     The Change Schedule of 'ScanDisk for Windows' window appears.

5   Under Run, click Daily.

     This sets ScanDisk to run each day.

6   Under Start At, select the text and type **12:10 pm**, and then click the Wait Until I
     Haven't Used My Computer For box.

7   Select the text in the Wait Until I Haven't Used My Computer For box and type **15**.

     This sets ScanDisk to run daily at ten minutes past noon, but only if you haven't
     been using your computer for 15 minutes.

8   Click the Settings button.

9   Under Select Drive(s) You Want To Check For Errors, select Drive C.

10   Click the Automatically Fix Errors check box to select it.

11   Click OK, and then click OK again.

     The settings are saved.

Modify a task

1   Use the right mouse button to click the last task in the Schedule Program list, (this
     is the task you added in the previous exercise) and then click Change Schedule.

2   Under Run, click Weekly.

3   Under Start At, select the text in the first box, and then type **7:00 pm**

4   Under Start At, click the Every down arrow and select Wednesday.

5   Click OK.

      The task settings are changed.

Deleting a task

1   Use the right mouse button to click the last task in the list, and then click Remove.

      The Are You Sure? window appears.

2   Click Yes.

      The task is removed.

3   On the System Agent window, click the Close box.

Using DriveSpace 3 for Maximum Disk Compression

Suppose you are working on your computer, and you discover that you are starting to run out of space on your hard disk. You can buy another hard disk, of course, or you can use the version of DriveSpace disk compression that comes with Windows 95 to increase the storage. But, the compression program that comes with Windows 95 can only create a maximum of 512 MB per compressed drive. If you have Microsoft Plus!, however, you can use DriveSpace 3, which can get even more compression on your hard disk and can create compressed drives up to 2 gigabytes in size.

Like DriveSpace that ships with Windows 95, DriveSpace 3 works in the background (the program is running, but no window appears to show you that the program is running), requiring no input from you, compressing and decompressing files as you save and open them.

 TIP   For more information on disk compression, see Lesson 3, "Compressing Your Hard Disk."

If you have a Pentium computer, you can have DriveSpace 3 perform high-level compression on your hard disk to get even more compression. UltraPack and HiPack compression are the names of DriveSpace 3 compression methods that provide maximum storage space on a disk. You need a Pentium processor to use these methods, because DriveSpace 3 must run continuously to achieve this high-level compression.

Start DriveSpace 3

In this exercise, you use DriveSpace 3 to compress 5 MB of space on your hard disk. This exercise assumes that you have a Pentium computer. You can try to do this exercise if you don't have a Pentium computer, but your computer might run extremely slowly.

NOTE This exercise is for demonstration purposes only. The exercise will direct you to use only 5 MB of free disk space. This is really too small an amount to be of any practical use. However, you can use the same procedure regardless of the amount of free space you decide to use. If you do decide to use all or most of the free space on your disk for this exercise, the compression process will probably take a considerable amount of time.

1 Click Start, point to Programs, point to Accessories, point to System Tools, and click DriveSpace.

DriveSpace 3 starts.

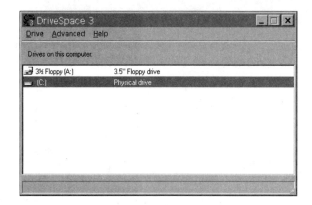

2 In the Drives On This Computer list, click Drive C.

3 On the Advanced menu, click Create Empty.

The Create New Compressed Drive Window appears. You will use this window to create a new drive using some of the empty space on drive C.

If you want to use most of the empty space on your hard disk, don't change the number that first appears in the Using box.

4 Select the text in the Using box, and then type **5**

This will create a new compressed drive using 5 MB of the free space on drive C.

5 Click Start.

DriveSpace 3 begins compressing the drive. If you have an Emergency Startup disk, which should have been created when you first installed Windows 95, you can have your Emergency Startup disk updated with information about DriveSpace 3. If you don't have an Emergency Startup disk, click Cancel when you're prompted to update your Emergency Startup disk. After a few moments, the Create New Compressed Drive dialog box reappears.

TROUBLESHOOTING If there are errors on your hard disk, you will be directed to use ScanDisk to correct those errors before DriveSpace 3 will continue.

6   Click Close.

The new drive is created. The DriveSpace Performance Tuning window appears.

7   On the DriveSpace Performance Tuning window, click the More Free Disk Space button.

This sets the option to get the highest compression and the most storage from the new compressed drive. The DriveSpace 3 window appears.

8   Click the Close button on the DriveSpace 3 window.

IMPORTANT Make certain that you close any programs you might be using before you click Yes in the next step.

9   Click Yes to restart your computer.

Verify the properties of the compressed drive

In this exercise you examine the properties of your new compressed disk drive. A compressed hard disk looks and acts just like any other hard disk in your system. The compression software takes care of the real work of compressing and decompressing files as you write and read them. Usually, you will not notice any performance degradation just from using disk compression software, with the exception of UltraPack and HiPack compression on non-Pentium computers.

1   Double-click My Computer, then double-click drive G, or whichever drive is the new compressed drive.

2   Use the right mouse button to click in the Drive G window and click Properties on the shortcut menu.

The Drive G Properties window appears.

3   Click the Compression tab to make it active.

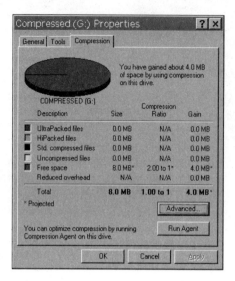

4 After viewing the properties, click the Close button.

5 Hold down SHIFT, and then click the Close button on the Drive G window.

Remove the compressed drive

1 Click Start, point to Programs, point to Accessories, point to System Tools, and click DriveSpace.

2 Select Drive G (the new compressed drive).

3 On the Drive menu, click Uncompress.

4 Click Start.

DriveSpace 3 begins uncompressing the drive. When the drive is uncompressed, the DriveSpace 3 window appears.

5 If the message box appears asking whether you want to remove the DriveSpace 3 compression driver from memory, click Yes.

6 Click Yes to restart Windows so that the uncompressing process can finish.

7 Click Close to restart Windows in its normal mode.

Windows restarts and the compressed drive (G) is no longer part of your system.

One Step Further: Finding the Easter Egg

The Easter egg (so called because you have to search for it and it's a surprise when you do find it) is a special feature of Microsoft Windows 95. The Easter egg for Windows 95 displays the names of The Microsoft Windows 95 Product Team! It has no practical application, but it can enhance the enjoyment of using Windows 95. The use of such

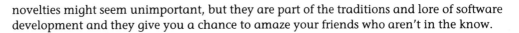

novelties might seem unimportant, but they are part of the traditions and lore of software development and they give you a chance to amaze your friends who aren't in the know.

Find the Windows 95 Easter egg

1   Use the right mouse button to click the Desktop, point to New, and then click Folder on the shortcut menu.

Be sure to enter all of the punctuation just as you see it here.

2   Type **and now, the moment you've all been waiting for** and then press ENTER.

3   Use the right mouse button to click the folder, and then click Rename on the shortcut menu. Type **we proudly present for your viewing pleasure** and then press ENTER.

4   Sorry, you'll have to figure out the last step on your own. After all, giving away all the answers would be cheating.

5   Once you have figured out the last step, double-click the folder to see the display.

If you want to continue to the next lesson

➤   Close all open windows.

If you want to quit Windows 95 for now

1   Close all open windows.

2   On the Start menu, click Shut Down, and then click Yes.

Lesson Summary

To	Do this
Install Microsoft Plus!	Insert the Microsoft Plus! CD in the CD-ROM drive and click Install.
Select a Desktop theme	Click Start, point to Settings, and click Control Panel. Double-click the Desktop Themes control panel. Select the theme you want to use and then click OK.
Use full window drag	Use the right mouse button to click the Desktop, and then click Properties on the shortcut menu. Click the Plus! tab and place a checkmark next to Show Window Contents While Dragging.

To	Do this
Use font smoothing	Use the right mouse button to click the Desktop, click Properties on the shortcut menu. Click the Plus! tab and place a checkmark next to Smooth Edges Of Screen Fonts.
Schedule a task in System Agent	Click the System Agent icon on the taskbar. Click Schedule A New Program on the Program menu. Fill in the dialog box with the program name, and then click When To Run. Fill in the dialog box and then click OK.
Use DriveSpace 3 for maximum disk compression	Click Start, point to Programs, point to Accessories, point to System Tools, and then click DriveSpace. Click Create Empty on the Advanced menu, or click Compress on the File menu.

For online information about	From the Help dialog box, click Index and then type
Working with full window drag	**Window, full-window drag**
Using font smoothing	**Font smoothing**
Using the System Agent	**System Agent, about System Agent**
Using DriveSpace 3	**DriveSpace 3, about enhanced disk compression**

Preview of the Next Lesson

In the next lesson, you'll learn how to use the networking features of Microsoft Plus! You'll install and use the Dial-Up Network Server to accept incoming calls to your network. You'll work with the Internet on The Microsoft Network, and you'll take a break playing 3-D Pinball.

Networking with Microsoft Plus!

Estimated time
40 min.

In this lesson you will learn how to:

- Set up and use the Dial-Up Networking server.
- Work with the Internet through The Microsoft Network.
- Relax with 3-D Pinball for Windows.

In this lesson, you'll learn how to use the networking features of Microsoft Plus! You'll install and use the Dial-Up Networking server to accept incoming calls to your network. You'll work with the Internet on The Microsoft Network, and you'll take a break playing 3-D Pinball for Windows.

Using the Dial-Up Networking Server

Suppose your assistant is on the road with her laptop computer, and she wants to use the network resources at your home office. She might want to copy a file from a computer in the home office to her laptop, modify the file, and then print the file on the network printer back at the home office for you to review. With the Dial-Up Networking server, a Windows 95 additional component that is included with Microsoft Plus! your assistant can connect to your home office network through her computer modem.

When you use Dial-Up Networking, you set up a list of users who are authorized to dial into your Dial-Up Networking server. If you use user-level access control, the list of authorized users is provided by your Windows NT domain or Novell NetWare server. If you use share-level access control, you can set up a password to grant access to the Dial-Up Networking server. (For information on access controls, see "Working with Network Resources," in Lesson 4.)

Because file and printer sharing is involved when you use Dial-Up Networking, you must install file and printer sharing service on each computer in your home office network to which you want to grant access. For example, if you have three networked computers, and you want to provide remote access to the files and printers on two of the computers, you must select file and printer sharing service for the two computers. (The third computer is still attached to the home office network, but remote users will not be able to access its resources.) You must use file and printer sharing service on each computer to which you want to grant access. If file and printer sharing service is not installed, see "Enabling File and Printer Sharing," in Lesson 4 for more information.

The Dial-Up Networking server controls the modem port and monitors incoming calls. When a remote computer calls into your home office computer, the Dial-Up Networking server answers the call. The remote user then enters the requested information in the login dialog box, and the Dial-Up Networking server verifies that the user has access to the network. If the user does not type the correct information, the Dial-Up Networking server terminates the call, and then waits for the next call.

NOTE   When the Dial-Up Networking server is waiting for a caller, it locks the modem from use by programs designed to run under earlier versions of Windows, such as CompuServe Information Manager for Windows, or America Online for Windows. You will have to disable the Dial-Up Networking server to use the modem with such programs. Programs that are designed for Windows 95, such as The Microsoft Network, will be able to use the modem, as long as the Dial-Up Networking server is just waiting for a caller and not actively being used by a remote computer.

Setting Up the Dial-Up Networking Server

You install the Dial-Up Networking server component from the Microsoft Plus! CD-ROM or from the installation floppy disks. It is part of the default installation when you choose the Typical installation option. If you use the Custom setup option, you can select the Dial-Up Networking server as a separate component.

In the following exercise, you set up the Dial-Up Networking server to answer the phone and verify authorized users. This exercise assumes that your assistant is using her remote computer to dial into your home office computer, which is part of your home office network. The computer you are setting up as a Dial-Up Networking server is assumed to be using File And Printer Sharing For Microsoft Networks.

Verify access settings

Before you set up the Dial-Up Networking server, you'll verify that the current network settings are set to the access you use—either share-level or user-level.

1   Use the right mouse button to click Network Neighborhood, and then click Properties.

2   Click the Configuration tab and verify that File And Printer Sharing For Microsoft Networks is installed.

    You might have to scroll to the bottom of the installed network components list box to find File And Printer Sharing For Microsoft Networks.

3   Click the Access Control tab, and verify that the access control settings are set to the access level you use—either share-level or user-level.

4   Click OK.

    The Network Neighborhood Properties window closes.

Set up the Dial-Up Networking server for share-level access

In this exercise, you set up the Dial-Up Networking server, and you establish a password for accessing the server. If you use user-level access, skip to the exercise, "Set Up the Dial-Up Networking server for User-Level Access."

1   Double-click My Computer.

2   Double-click Dial-Up Networking.

    If the Welcome To Dial-Up Networking dialog box appears, click Cancel.

3   On the Connections menu, click Dial-Up Server.

    The Dial-Up Server window opens.

4   Click the Allow Caller Access option, and then click Apply.

    The Dial-Up Networking Server is enabled. The Status box displays "Monitoring."

5 Click the Change Password button.

The Dial-Up Networking Password dialog box appears.

The password you establish here is for dial-up networking access. You can establish additional passwords for each shared resource if you are using share-level access control.

6 In the New Password box, type **!Win95!** and in the Confirm New Password box type **!Win95!**

The password you type is the one that will be used by the remote user to access the home office network. After calling into your computer, anyone who knows the password can connect to your network, so it's a good idea to choose a different password than the startup Windows logon password used to access Windows 95.

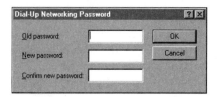

7 Click OK.

The new password is established.

8 Click OK again.

Holding down SHIFT while clicking the Close button automatically closes a series of subfolder windows.

9 Hold down SHIFT and click the Close button on the Dial-Up Networking Server window.

The Dial-Up Networking Server window and the My Computer window close.

Set up the Dial-Up Networking server for user-level access

In this exercise, you set up the Dial-Up Networking server, and you select valid users who can access the server.

1 Double-click My Computer.

2 Double-click Dial-Up Networking.

If the Welcome To Dial-Up Networking window appears, click Cancel.

3 On the Connections menu, click Dial-Up Server.

The Dial-Up Server window opens.

4 Click the Allow Caller Access option, and then click Apply.

The Dial-Up Networking Server is enabled. The Status box displays "Idle."

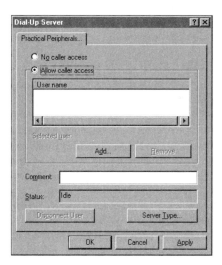

5 Click the Add button.

The Add Users dialog box appears.

6 In the Name list, select a user, and then click Add.

The name is added to the list of valid users.

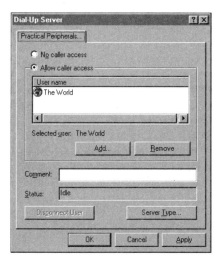

7 Click OK.

The user is accepted.

Holding down SHIFT while clicking the Close button automatically closes a series of subfolder windows.

8 Hold down SHIFT and click the Close button on the Dial-Up Networking Server window.

The Dial-Up Networking Server window and the My Computer window close.

Monitoring Remote Network Connections

Now that you've set up the Dial-Up Networking server on your computer, suppose that you'd like to monitor the calls you receive. You can use the Dial-Up Networking server to monitor the calls on your home office computer that's attached to the home office network.

In the next exercise, you monitor the status of a remote network connection on your computer. This exercise assumes that you have a computer connected to a network, that the computer has the Dial-Up Networking server installed and enabled, that a modem is connected to the computer that can accept outside calls, and that a remote user is dialing into the computer.

 NOTE It isn't necessary to have the Dial-Up Networking server connected to a network. You can establish a remote connection to a standalone computer using the same procedures. The standalone computer, however, will still have to be using file and printer sharing for the remote computer to have access to any of the dial-up server's resources.

Monitor a remote call

1 Double-click My Computer, and then double-click Dial-Up Networking.

The Dial-Up Networking window opens.

2 On the Connections menu, click Dial-Up Server, click Allow Caller Access, and then wait for a call from a remote user.

3 When the remote user calls, view the information in the Status box.

The Status box displays information about who is calling when the remote user connects.

4 When the remote user hangs up, click the OK button.

The Dial-Up Server window closes.

5 Hold down SHIFT and click the Close button on the Dial-Up Networking window.

The Dial-Up Networking window and the My Computer window close.

Disabling Access Through the Dial-Up Networking Server

You can disable dial-up access to your network by using the Dial-Up Networking server. After you disable access, no one can access any resources through your computer.

Disable access

In this exercise, you disable dial-up access to your computer and the home office network as well.

1   Double-click My Computer, and then double-click Dial-Up Networking.

2   On the Connections menu, click Dial-Up Server.

3   Click the No Caller Access option.

Clicking No Caller Access disables access to your computer and the home office network.

4   Click OK.

The Dial-Up Server window closes.

5   Hold down SHIFT and click the Close button on the Dial-Up Networking window.

The Dial-Up Networking window and the My Computer window close.

Working with the Internet Through The Microsoft Network

You can use The Microsoft Network to work directly with the Internet, a world-wide "network of networks" that connects many educational institutions, research organizations, businesses, governments, and even private individuals. The Internet contains resources you can use to research topics, purchase airplane tickets, send flowers, read the latest movie reviews, and many other activities. The Internet is dynamic—each day, hundreds of new users and new sites sign on. And the Internet reaches across the world. You might be browsing through a site in Great Britain, and then, with just one click of the mouse, jump to another site in New Zealand, Kenya, or even Antarctica.

The Internet: The Early Years

The Internet started out in the 1970s as the ARPANET, a network project of the United States Defense Department. The ARPANET included sites such as defense installations, research institutes, and educational institutions. These sites were interconnected through a link to one of the ARPANET supercomputers.

At each site, users could sign on and immediately begin using the network to exchange information. Various sites around the country began collecting information for users to view. Many sites contained libraries of information for research. As the number of these sites grew, catalogs of information were developed. Users could search through the catalogs to find the materials they wanted. One popular catalog search program from the University of Minnesota, known as Gopher, became a standard tool for browsing through and finding information. Gopher presented the information in an organized series of menus; however, the information was in text-only format.

When users found an item they wanted to retrieve, they had to have a program that could transfer the file from the remote location to their local computer. The FTP program, short for File Transfer Protocol, was developed to transfer these files. With Gopher and FTP, as well as other specialized tools, the ARPANET became a widely-used and dependable tool for research and communication.

Still, the ARPANET was limited to military, research, and educational uses. The network gained wide acceptance for its audience, but commercial and recreational use was forbidden. Educational and other non-profit research institutions soon found out that the ARPANET was an efficient tool to transmit non-defense–related information. Researchers, students, and other users developed programs to work with the Internet that would allow users to access research databases at remote sites and send mail electronically.

Connections to other countries and continents were opened, and soon researchers in many countries began exchanging information. Other networks, both in the United States and in other countries, were connected to the ARPANET, and the ARPANET became part of a larger collection of networks.

In the late 1980s, uses and users of the ARPANET slowly began to increase; however, it was still limited to non-commercial communications. After a few more years, the ARPANET supercomputers themselves were retired, and new supercomputers were used to connect the Internet sites. Eventually, the Defense Department transferred its ownership and maintenance to a separate, non-profit group, and the ARPANET became the Internet.

Using the Internet Today

In 1991, the Internet was opened to the public, and Internet use began to increase dramatically as more and more networks became connected to each other, and more and more sites and users signed on. By the mid-1990s, it was estimated that there were between 5 and 30 million users in the United States alone. Now anyone who can call an Internet access provider (also called an Internet service provider) through his or her modem can access the Internet. Internet access providers provide the link between the Internet user and the Internet supercomputers. The Microsoft Network is one such Internet access provider. You can use The Microsoft Network to view the resources on the Internet.

One main resource on the Internet is its newsgroups. Internet newsgroups are a collection of related discussions and documents on a specific topic or theme, such as political debates or biotechnology research. Newsgroups are one method used to disseminate information on the Internet. But newsgroups can only display text messages.

In the last few years, another method was developed for research called the World Wide Web, or Web. The Web is composed of Web pages, which are individual documents that can contain text, graphics, sound, and other elements. You need a Web browser, such as the Microsoft Internet Explorer that is shown in the following illustration, to view Web pages on your screen.

One benefit of using The Microsoft Network and the Internet Explorer together is that you can view information on The Microsoft Network and the Internet as if they were both one seamless environment.

In the following sections of this lesson, you'll learn more about newsgroups and the Web, and how to access these resources on the Internet.

NOTE Although there is a central resource in the United States that oversees the operation of the Internet, it's important to realize that no one person or organization owns, manages, or sets policies for the Internet. The following information about newsgroups and Web sites describes the conventions used on the Internet rather than the rules.

Using Internet Newsgroups

One type of newsgroup on the Internet is the Usenet newsgroups. These newsgroups are similar to bulletin board systems on The Microsoft Network—they contain messages and responses about a particular topic. For example, if you want to review discussions about backcountry hiking, you could browse through a newsgroup devoted to that topic. You can read a set of related messages and responses collected in a *thread* (a *conversation* on The Microsoft Network) on a newsgroup. You can post a reply to a message, or create a new message.

Newsgroups can be *moderated* or *unmoderated*. The contents of moderated newsgroups are reviewed by the owner of the newsgroup before the messages are posted. The contents of unmoderated newsgroups are posted as soon as a message is sent to the newsgroup. Usually moderated newsgroups are more coherent than unmoderated newsgroups; however, messages appear more slowly in moderated newsgroups, because someone must review each message before it is posted.

As of October 1995, there were over 10,000 newsgroups worldwide. You can find newsgroups on just about any subject you want. These newsgroups are usually divided in up to eight general-interest areas as follows.

Newsgroup area	Topic discussed
comp	Computers, computer science, hardware, and software
humanities	Fine arts, literature, history, and other humanities
misc	Miscellaneous topics not covered by the other topics
news	News about Internet newsgroups
rec	Recreation and hobbies
sci	Science, scientific research, applications, and related issues
soc	Social issues, politics, and related issues
talk	A variety of topics, usually controversial

On The Microsoft Network, you can also access other newsgroups, such as alt, bionet or biz, by opening the Categories\Internet Center\Internet Newsgroups\How To Access All Newsgroups folder, and then filling out the Full Newsgroups Access Form. The alt newsgroup contains the alternative newsgroups and cover a variety of topics not usually covered in any other newsgroup. The bionet newsgroup contains information on biology and related topics. The biz newsgroup contains information that is more commercial than most of the other Usenet newsgroups.

Other newsgroups that are part of the Internet but are not included as Usenet newsgroups can also be viewed by using The Microsoft Network. You can view these newsgroups in the Categories\Internet Center\Internet Newsgroups\NetNews forum.

TIP To access the NetNews forum, use the right mouse button to click The Microsoft Network icon in the taskbar, click Go To, type **netnews** in the Type A Go Word For A Particular Service box, and then click OK.

Each newsgroup is located on a remote computer attached to the Internet, and is not maintained by The Microsoft Network. When you browse through a newsgroup, The Microsoft Network provides you with access to the newsgroup. For example, the following illustration shows a list of backcountry topics within the recreation newsgroup.

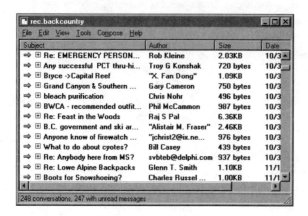

Each newsgroup is organized into hierarchies. For example, under comp you might find comp.databases, a discussion of databases, and comp.networks, a discussion of networking and computers. In the hierarchy of messages, the name of each subgroup of the main group is separated from each other name by a period, but in spoken conversation the word "dot" is used. For example, news.newusers.questions would be the questions group in the newusers group in the news group. For more help about using the Internet, use the topic Internet Newsgroups, Frequently Asked Questions in the Help Topics window of The Microsoft Network.

TIP If you would like to get more information about creating Newsgroups, type **ftp://rtfm.mit.edu/pub/usenet/news.groups** in the Address box of the Internet Explorer, press ENTER, and then click the phrase How_to_Create_a_New_Usenet_Newsgroup.

Opening a Newsgroup with the Internet Center

The Internet Center contains a set of jumping-off points to other areas on the Internet, as well as information kiosks, an Internet bulletin board service (BBS) for discussing the Internet, and other information about using The Microsoft Network with the Internet.

To open a newsgroup and read its messages, you open the Internet Center, and then open the Usenet newsgroup.

NOTE The content of any newsgroup is not restricted except in a moderated discussion, and can contain objectionable material. There is no central governing authority for the Internet. If you do not want to read material about some topics, you should avoid newsgroups that discuss those topics. The Microsoft Network has no ability to restrict the content of any newsgroup, and cannot delete messages.

Open the Internet Center

In this exercise, you start The Microsoft Network and then open the Internet Center.

The Microsoft Network

1 Double-click The Microsoft Network icon.

2 In the Member ID box, type your name. In the Password box, type your password.

   If you previously logged onto The Microsoft Network, your Member ID should already be displayed in the text box.

3 Click Connect.

   It will take a few moments for the modem connection to be established.

4 When The Microsoft Network window appears, click Categories.

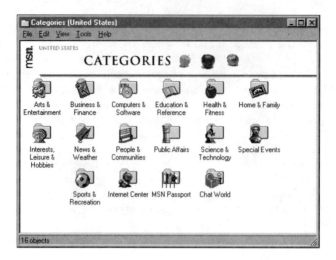

5 In the Categories window, double-click the Internet Center icon.

The Internet Center window appears.

6 In the Internet Center window, double-click Internet Newsgroups.

The Internet Newsgroups window appears.

7 Double-click Usenet Newsgroups.

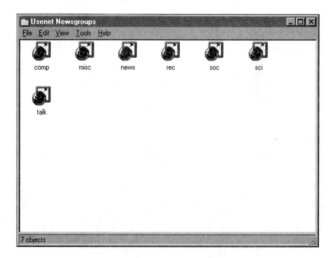

View the contents of a newsgroup

In this exercise, you'll view information about Windows 95, which is located in the comp (computer-related) newsgroup.

1 Double-click comp to open the comp newsgroup.

2 Double-click the following folders to get to the Windows 95 information in the comp newsgroup
comp.os
comp.os.ms-windows
comp.os.ms-windows.win95

3 Double-click comp.os.ms-windows.win95.misc.

The list of messages about Windows 95 appears.

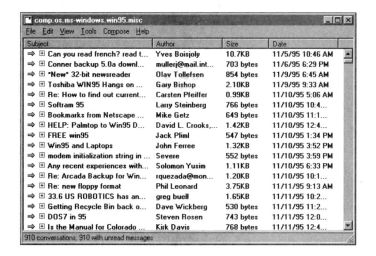

Read a message

1 Scroll through the messages.

2 When you find a message of interest, double-click it.

The message opens.

3 After reading the message, click the Close button on the message window.

The message closes.

Posting a message to a newsgroup

In the following exercise, you post a message to the newsgroup news.newusers.questions. This newsgroup is for new newsgroup users to practice posting messages.

 NOTE   You can only read and post messages to newsgroups using The Microsoft Network. You cannot create new groups, nor can you delete posted messages, even your own.

Post a message

1   On the View menu, click Toolbars.

The Toolbar appears.

2   Click the Go To A Different Folder down arrow.

3   Click Usenet Newsgroups.

The Usenet Newsgroups window appears.

4   Double-click the following folders to go to the news.newusers newsgroup.
news
news.newusers
news.newusers.questions

The list of messages in the news.newusers.questions group appears.

New Message

5   Click the New Message button.

The New Message window appears.

6   In the Subject box, type **Windows 95**

7   In the message area, type **Windows 95 Is Great! It's Better Than Chocolate Cake!**

Post

8   Click the Post button.

9   Use the right mouse button to click an open area on the taskbar, and then click Minimize All on the shortcut menu.

Browsing Through the World Wide Web

You can also browse through Web pages, which are locations on the Internet that combine text and graphics to display information in an attractive format. You use a Web browser to view Web pages and view information that combines text, graphics, and increasingly, audio and video. With a Web browser, you can "browse" through a collection of multimedia data and pick and choose as you go.

Web pages can also be used to collect information from a user and transmit the information to another site. For example, you might browse through a Web page that contains a product catalog or a schedule of classes. To order a product or service, you would fill out a form on-screen, and then click a button to transmit your order to the distribution center. For example, the following illustration shows a form you can fill out to receive a schedule of classes.

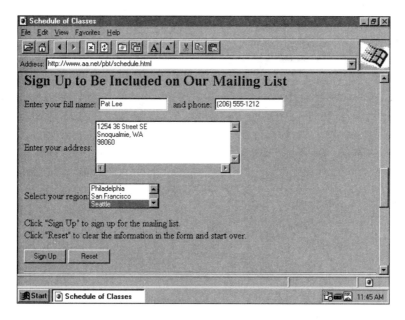

The real benefit of Web pages, however, are the jumps to other documents. These jumps, also called hypertext jumps, can take you from a document in Illinois to a document in Vienna with just a click of the mouse. For example, the following illustration shows a page from The Microsoft Network that provides jumps to other topics. Jumps to other Web pages usually appear as underlined phrases or words. You simply click the phrase or word to jump to, or go to, the Web page on that topic.

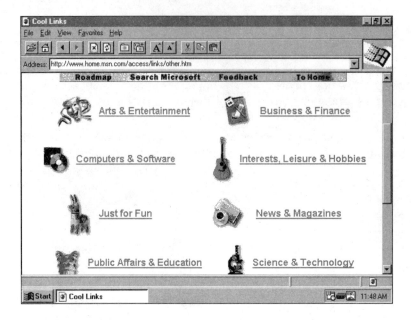

Some sophisticated Web pages combine pictures and jumps as *clickable maps*. A clickable map is a picture that contains areas which, when clicked, jump to another page on the Web. For example, a picture of a world map could have countries that, when clicked, take you to specific information about the country you clicked.

Each page on the Web is identified by its Universal Resource Locator, or URL. You can use the URL to find that page on the Web. For example, the URL to the main page at Microsoft is http://www.microsoft.com. The prefix http:// stands for HyperText Transfer Protocol. If the http:// prefix is not used in the URL, the Web browser won't find that page.

Every Web page is stored at a Web site, which is the physical location for the Web page. For example, the Web pages www.microsoft.com/Misc/ShortCuts.htm and www.microsoft.com/corpinfo/HotTopics.htm are different pages stored at the same Web site, www.microsoft.com.

Explore the Web with the Internet Explorer

In the following exercise, you explore the Web by using the Internet Explorer. You'll go to the main Microsoft Web page, go to another location using a clickable map, and then explore a third location using a jump.

Internet Explorer

1   Double-click the Internet Explorer icon.

The Internet Explorer starts.

2   In the Address box, type **http://www.microsoft.com**, which is the URL address to the main Microsoft Web page.

NOTE The path to any part of the Web is case-sensitive. The URL www.website.com/Intro.htm and www.website.com/intro.htm refer to two different pages. When typing an address in the Address box, be careful to use the correct case.

3 Press ENTER.

The Internet Explorer begins searching for the main Microsoft Web page. After a few moments, the main page appears in the Internet Explorer window.

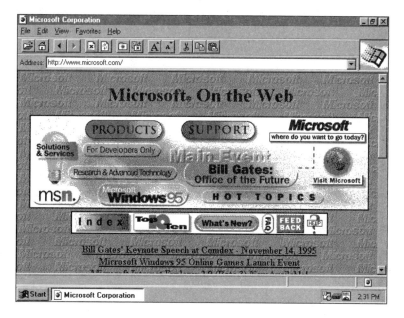

4 Click the word Index on the first picture to jump to the Index Web page.

The picture is a clickable map. The Web page appears in the Internet Explorer window.

5 Click any of the blue underlined phrases.

The blue underlined phrases are jumps that take you to another page on the Internet.

6 Click the Back button.

The previous page reappears in the Internet Explorer window.

7 Click the Address down arrow.

A list of previously-visited sites appears in the Address list.

Back

8 Press ESCAPE, and then click the File menu.

Pressing ESCAPE closes the drop-down list. The list of previously-visited pages appears in the File menu.

9 In the File list, click Microsoft Corporation.

The main Web page for Microsoft Corporation appears in the Internet Explorer window again.

Saving a Favorite Web Page

One of the main frustrations in working with the Internet is remembering the address of the Web page you visited last week. You might browse for several hours, but after you leave your computer, you can't find the same Web pages.

You can store the addresses of your favorite Web pages in the Favorites folder. When you find a page you'd like to revisit, you store its URL; then, when you want to revisit the page, you open the stored URL to reopen the Web page.

Save a page in the Favorites folder

In this exercise, you store a URL in the Favorites folder, and then you use the Favorites folder to revisit a Web site.

1 On the Favorites menu, click Add To Favorites, and then click Add.

The current URL, www.microsoft.com, is saved to the Favorites folder.

2 Click the Visit The Microsoft Network icon in the clickable map, or click the blue underlined phrase MSN further down the page.

The main page to The Microsoft Network appears.

3 Click the Favorites menu.

A list of favorite locations appears. The locations are listed alphabetically by title.

4 Click the entry for Microsoft Corporation.

The main Web page for Microsoft Corporation appears.

Close the Internet connection

When you are finished using the Internet, you can close your connection by closing The Microsoft Network.

1 Use the right mouse button to click The Microsoft Network icon in the taskbar.

2 Click Sign Out.

The Microsoft Network dialog box appears.

3 Click Yes.

The Microsoft Network closes.

Close the Internet Explorer

➤ Click the Close button on the Internet Explorer window.

The Internet Explorer closes.

Relaxing with 3-D Pinball for Windows

It's been a busy day, and you're ready to relax. You can use the 3-D Pinball for Windows game provided with Microsoft Plus! to relax. This game is a simulation of a true-to-life pinball machine. If you have a sound card with speakers attached to your computer, you can also hear realistic sounds from a pinball machine.

Play 3-D Pinball for Windows

In this exercise, you start 3-D Pinball for Windows, and then play a game.

1 Click Start, point to Programs, point to Accessories, point to Games then click Space Cadet Table.

The 3-D Pinball for Windows game starts and loads the Space Cadet Table layout.

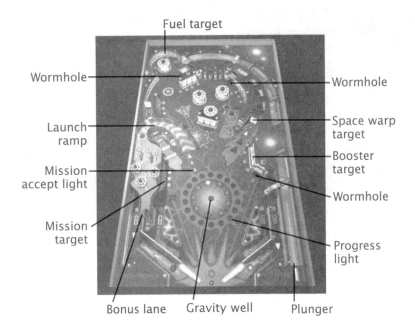

Fuel target

Wormhole

Wormhole

Launch ramp

Space warp target

Booster target

Mission accept light

Wormhole

Mission target

Progress light

Bonus lane   Gravity well   Plunger

You can also click Launch Ball on the File menu to begin playing.

2 Hold the SPACEBAR down to "pull" the plunger.

As you continue holding down the SPACEBAR, the plunger is pulled further down below the ball.

3 Release the SPACEBAR.

The ball is projected into the playing field of the 3-D Pinball for Windows game.

The <, >, and UP ARROW keys can nudge the table left, right, and up respectively.

4 Use the Z and / keys to activate the left and right flippers.

5 After you have played the first ball, you can use the SPACEBAR to play the next two balls. After you've played three balls, the game is over.

6 If the High Score window appears, type your name in the Name box, and then click OK.

The high score is entered. The game pauses. Press F2 to play another game.

You can earn additional bonus balls when you score.

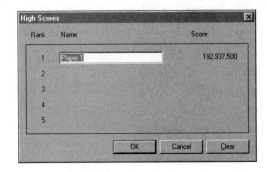

Changing Your Game Options

You can change the options for 3-D Pinball for Windows. For example, you can turn on the sound, change the keys used to play the game, or select from one to four players to participate in the game.

In the following exercises, you turn on the sound and music, change the keys used to play the game, and then switch to a two-player game.

Change the sound and music options

1 On the Options menu, click Sounds, if the option is not selected.

Sounds are now turned on and will play when you begin playing the game.

2 On the Options menu, click Music, if the option is not selected.

Music is now turned on and will play while you are playing the game.

Change the keys used to play the game

You can also press F8 to activate the Player Controls dialog box.

1 On the Options menu, click Player Controls.

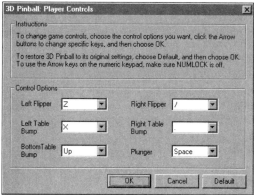

2 Press the Plunger down arrow.

A list of keys that can be used to pull down the plunger appears.

3 Scroll downward and click Down.

Clicking Down changes the key used to pull down the plunger to the Down arrow key.

4 Click OK.

The key is changed.

Change to a two-player game

▶ On the Options menu, point to Select Players, and then click 2 Players.

The game is set to play two players.

 TIP You can get more detailed information on strategies for playing Space Cadet 3D Pinball by reading the Pinball.doc file that is located in the 3D Pinball folder inside the Microsoft Plus! folder, which is, in turn, inside the Program Files folder.

Play the game with the new options

1 Press the DOWN arrow, and then release it when the plunger is pulled down as far as you want.

The DOWN arrow is the key you set to pull the plunger. When you release it, the ball is projected into the playing field. Because you changed the Sound option, each time the ball hits an object or you press the flippers, sounds are played on the speakers.

2 Play the first ball in the first round. When you are finished with the first ball, then your opponent can play the next ball in the first round.

3 Continue to play the game. When you have completed the game, you can enter your name and your opponent's name in the High Scores dialog box.

Closing the Game

When you have finished playing the game, you can close it. Closing the game closes the window. The high scores are retained until you play the next game and beat the scores, or until you clear the scores.

Close the game

▶ Click the Close button on the 3-D Pinball for Windows – Space Cadet window.

The game closes.

One Step Further: Creating an Internet Shortcut on the Desktop

You can store addresses to Internet locations in the Favorites folder in the Internet Explorer. You can also place shortcuts to Internet addresses on the Desktop. When you double-click the shortcut, The Microsoft Network and the Internet Explorer will start, and then the Internet address referred to in the shortcut will appear.

Create a shortcut to a main Web page

In this exercise, you create a shortcut to the main Web page at Microsoft Corporation, and then you use the shortcut to open the main Web page at Microsoft Corporation.

1   Use the right mouse button to click the Desktop, point to New, and click Shortcut.

    A new shortcut is created, and the Create Shortcut dialog box appears.

2   In the Command Line box, type **http://www.microsoft.com**

    This is the address for the main Web page at Microsoft Corporation.

3   Click Next.

    The Select A Title For The Program dialog box appears.

4   Select the text in the Select A Name For The Shortcut Box, and type **Microsoft Corporation**

    The name is changed to Microsoft Corporation.

5   Click Finish.

    The new shortcut is renamed and placed on the Desktop.

Use the shortcut to open its Web page

1   Double-click the Microsoft Corporation shortcut.

    The Internet Explorer window opens, and begins looking for a connection to the Internet. Because you don't have an active Internet connection yet, the Internet Explorer starts The Microsoft Network, and The Microsoft Network Sign In dialog box appears.

2   Verify that your name and password are correct, and then click Connect.

    After a few moments, your modem connection is established, and the main Web page to Microsoft Corporation appears in the Internet Explorer window.

3   View the information in the Internet Explorer window.

4   After you've viewed the information, click the Close button on the Internet Explorer window.

    The Internet Explorer window closes. The Microsoft Network dialog box appears to prompt you to disconnect from The Microsoft Network.

5   Click Yes.

    You are disconnected from The Microsoft Network.

If you want to continue to the next lesson

➤   Close all open windows.

If you want to quit Windows 95 for now

1 Close all open windows.

2 On the Start menu, click Shut Down, and then click Yes.

Lesson Summary

To	Do this
Set up a Dial-Up Networking server	Double-click My Computer. Double-click Dial-Up Networking. On the Connections menu, click Dial-Up Server. Click the Allow Caller Access Button, and then click Apply.
Change the Dial-Up Networking password	Click the Change Password button. In the New Password box, type the new password. In the Confirm New Password box, retype the new password. Click OK.
Browse Internet newsgroups	Start The Microsoft Network. Double-click Categories, double-click Internet Center, and then double-click Usenet Newsgroups. Double-click the newsgroup you want to read. Double-click the message you want to read. When you're finished reading the message, click the Close button on the message window, and then click the Close button on The Microsoft Network window.

To	Do this
Browse Internet Web pages	Double-click the Internet Explorer icon. In the Address box, type an Internet address, and press ENTER. Click a spot on a clickable map, or, click any jump on the Web page that appears.
Play 3-D Pinball for Windows	Click Start, point to Programs, point to Accessories, point to Games, point to 3-D Pinball for Windows, and then click Space Cadet Table. Press SPACEBAR to project the ball into the playing field. Press Z and / to use the flippers. Click the Close button to close the window.

For more information on	From the Help dialog box, click Index and then type
Using the Dial-Up Networking server	**dial-up server, setting up**
Browsing through the Internet	**browsing, through the Internet**
Playing 3-D Pinball for Windows	**Pinball game**

Review & Practice

In the lessons in Part 4, you learned how to work with Microsoft Plus! If you want to practice these skills and test your understanding, you can work through the Review & Practice section following this lesson.

Review & Practice

You will review and practice how to:

Estimated time
25 min.

- Modify the appearance of Windows 95.
- Schedule tasks by using the System Agent.
- Use DriveSpace 3 for maximum disk compression.
- Access the Internet through The Microsoft Network.
- Relax with 3-D Pinball.

Before you finish this book, you can practice the skills you learned in Part 4 by working through the steps in this Review & Practice section.

Scenario

Now that you have successfully set up the computers in your home office, you have decided to use the features of Microsoft Plus! to enhance the operation and appearance of Windows 95, such as changing the appearance of your Desktop, browsing through the Internet, and using the System Agent to schedule the task of running ScanDisk when you restart Windows 95.

Step 1: Modify the Appearance of the Desktop

Use Desktop themes to modify the appearance of your Desktop.

1 Start Desktop Themes.

2 In the Themes window, select a new theme.

For more information on	See
Selecting a Desktop theme	Lesson 10

Step 2: Use System Agent to Schedule a Task

Now that you have changed the Desktop theme, use the System Agent to schedule the task of running ScanDisk.

1 Open the System Agent window.

2 Add the ScanDisk for Windows program (scandskw.exe) to the list of scheduled programs.

3 In the Description box, type a description for this task.

4 Set the program to run at startup. (Hint: Click the When To Run button, and then click the At Startup option.)

5 Close the System Agent window.

For more information on	See
Using System Agent	Lesson 10
Scheduling a task	Lesson 10

Step 3: Use DriveSpace 3 for Maximum Compression

Now that you've set up a task in System Agent, you'll compress your disk by using DriveSpace 3. Use 8 MB of the empty space on Drive C.

Start DriveSpace 3

1 From the Tools menu in Accessories, click DriveSpace 3.

2 Select drive C and set DriveSpace to use 8 MB of free space. (Hint: On the Advanced menu, click Create Empty. In the Using box, type 8.)

3 Start DriveSpace to begin the compression.

4 On the DriveSpace Performance Tuning window, click the More Free Disk Space button.

5 Close the DriveSpace 3 window, and then restart Windows 95 to run ScanDisk.

Verify the properties of the compressed drive

1 Open the new compressed drive.

2 On the shortcut menu, click Properties. Review the properties of the compressed drive.

3 Close the dialog box, and then close the drive window.

For more information on	See
Using DriveSpace 3	Lesson 10
Compressing a drive	Lesson 10

Step 4: *Work with the Internet Through The Microsoft Network*

After compressing the drive, access the Internet by using The Microsoft Network.

1 Open the Internet Explorer.

2 Connect to The Microsoft Network.

3 In the Address box, type **http://www.msn.com** and press ENTER.

This is the URL to The Microsoft Network main page.

4 Click one of the jumps on The Microsoft Network main page, and then jump to another site on the Internet.

5 When you have finished browsing through the Internet, close the Internet Explorer window.

6 Disconnect from The Microsoft Network.

For more information on	See
Browsing the Internet	Lesson 11
Using the Internet Explorer	Lesson 11

Step 5: *Relax with 3-D Pinball*

To round out your Review & Practice, you can play 3-D Pinball.

1 From the Games menu in Accessories, start 3-D Pinball.

2 Hold down and then release SHIFT to project a ball. Press Z and the forward slash (/) to keep the ball in play.

3 After you've played the last ball, type your name in the High Scores dialog box and then close it.

4 Close the 3-D Pinball window.

For more information on	See
Playing 3-D Pinball	Lesson 11

Finish the Review & Practice

1 Close all open windows by clicking the Close button.

2 If any window is minimized, use the right mouse button to click the window's taskbar button, and then click Close.

3 If you are finished using Windows 95 for now, on the Start menu click Shut Down, and then click Yes.

Appendix

Running MS-DOS and Windows 3.1 Programs

Estimated time
40 min.

In this appendix you will learn how to:

- Work with MS-DOS–based programs.
- Work with Windows 3.1–based programs.

Suppose you have successfully set up the computers in your home office. Because of your increasing skills with Windows 95, you've been asked to set up for your co-workers some older programs that were originally designed to run in MS-DOS and Windows 3.1.

In this appendix, you'll learn how to work with MS-DOS–based and Windows 3.1-based programs.

Working with MS-DOS–Based Programs

MS-DOS is the basis for many computer programs still in use today. Most MS-DOS–based programs will run under Windows 95. In the next exercises, you'll create a folder for your MS-DOS–based programs, install an MS-DOS–based program, and then create a shortcut for the program. If you are already using an MS-DOS–based program on your computer, you can skip to the section "Create an MS-DOS–based program shortcut."

Install MS-DOS–based program files

1   Double-click My Computer, and then double-click Drive C.

The window for Drive C appears.

2   Use the right mouse button to click a blank area in the Drive C window, point to New, and then click Folder.

3   Type **Database**, and then press ENTER.

It's a good idea to keep your folder filenames eight characters or less when you use MS-DOS–based programs.

4   In the Drive C window, double-click the More Windows SBS Practice folder.

You'll need to locate the folder if you installed the practice files to a different directory other than the default.

5   Double-click the Exercise folder.

The Exercise window appears.

6   Use the right mouse button to click Db, and then click Copy on the shortcut menu.

If you are installing a commercial MS-DOS–based program, you can usually start the installation of the program by double-clicking the Install or Setup utility that comes with the program.

7   Double-click the Database folder. Use the right mouse button to click a blank area in the window, and then click Paste.

8   Close the windows to My Computer, Drive C, More Windows SBS Practice, and Database.

Create an MS-DOS–based program shortcut

After you've installed the MS-DOS–based program, you can create an easy way to start the program. In this exercise, you create a new program group for the Db program you just installed, and then you create a shortcut for the Db program in the program group folder.

1   Click the Start menu, point to Settings, and then click Taskbar.

The Taskbar Properties dialog box appears.

2   Click the Start Menu Programs tab, and then click Advanced.

3   Under All Folders, click the Programs icon.

4   Use the right mouse button to click a blank area of the window under Contents of 'Programs', point to New, and then click Folder.

5   Type **My Programs**, and press ENTER.

You've now created your new program group called My Programs.

6   Double-click the My Programs icon.

The My Programs folder opens.

7   In the My Programs folder, use the right mouse button to click in the window, Point to New, click Shortcut, and then click the Browse button.

8   In the Browse window, open the Database folder, and then double-click the Db icon. Click Next.

9 In the Select A Name For The Program box, type **Database** and then click Next.

10 In the Select An Icon window, select the icon in the second row from the top, the third icon from the left, and then click Finish.

Your shortcut called Database is now created in the My Programs folder.

11 On the Explorer window, click the Close button.

Run the MS-DOS–based program

1 On the Start menu, point to Programs, point to My Programs, and then click Database.

2 After viewing the information, press ESC.

Installing a Windows 3.1-Based Program

Suppose you've upgraded to Windows 95, but you're still using some older Windows 3.1-based programs. Because Windows 95 was designed to run older Windows 3.1-based programs as well as newer Windows 95-based programs, you can run most Windows 3.1-based programs without any problems. If you have a Windows 3.1-based program already installed on your computer with a program icon in a program group, the Windows 95 installation will convert the Windows 3.1-based program group to a Windows 95-based program group, and it will convert the Windows 3.1-based program icon to a Windows 95 shortcut. If, however, you install Windows 95 to a separate directory, you will have to re-install any Windows 3.1-based programs you want to use in Windows 95.

Copy the Windows 3.1 program file to your computer

In this exercise, you'll create a program group and a shortcut for a Windows 3.1-based application. If you already have the Windows 3.1-based program installed on your computer, you can skip to the section "Creating a shortcut to a Windows 3.1-based application."

1 Double-click My Computer, and then double-click Drive C.

2 Use the right mouse button to click a blank area in the Drive C window, point to New on the shortcut menu, and then click Folder.

3 Type **Win31**, and then press ENTER.

It's a good idea to keep folder names to eight characters or less when you work with Windows 3.1-based programs.

4 Insert the More Windows SBS Practice files disk in Drive A or B.

5 Switch to the My Computer window, and then double-click Drive A or B.

6 Use the right mouse button to click Hello, and then click Copy on the shortcut menu.

239

7 Double-click the Win31 folder. Use the right mouse button to click a blank area, and then click Paste on the shortcut menu.

8 Close the windows for My Computer, Drive A or B, and Win31.

Create a shortcut to a Windows 3.1-based application

1 On the Start menu, point to Settings, and then click Taskbar.

The Taskbar Properties dialog box appears.

2 Click the Start Menu Programs tab, and then click Advanced.

3 Double-click the Programs icon, and then double-click the My Programs folder.

4 In the My Programs folder, use the right mouse button to click in the window.

5 Point to New, click Shortcut, and then click the Browse button.

6 In the Browse window, double-click the Win31 folder, and then double-click the Hello icon. Click Next.

7 In the Select A Name For The Program box, type **My Greeting Program** and then click Next.

8 On the Explorer window, click the Close button.

Run the Windows 3.1-based application

1 On the Start menu, point to Programs, point to My Programs, and then click My Greeting Program.

2 After viewing the greeting, click Exit.

If you want to quit Windows 95 for now

1 Close all open windows.

2 Remove the More Windows SBS Practice files disk from Drive A or B.

3 On the Start menu, click Shut Down, and then click Yes.

This glossary contains definitions of terms used in *More Windows 95 Step by Step*. For definitions of additional terms, see Windows 95 online Help.

accessories   Basic programs included with Windows 95 that assist you with your everyday work on the computer, for example, WordPad and Paint. Accessories also include utilities that help you use your computer's telecommunication, fax, and multimedia capabilities more easily. System tools are accessories that help you manage your computer resources. Games are also included as part of your Windows 95 accessories.

application   *See* program.

back up   To create a duplicate copy of files to ensure against loss or damage.

backup disk   A disk that contains information copied from another disk or drive.

bad sector   A defect in the physical area of a disk that renders the sector unusable for storing data.

bulletin board service (BBS)   A computer service that is usually set up for a specific audience or purpose, such as members of professional organizations or people searching for a job. Members who call the bulletin board service using a computer and a modem can read and send messages, do research, post and read general announcements, and more. On The Microsoft Network, a bulletin board is a set of collected messages and responses from its users on various related topics, such as sports, finance, culture, and so on.

CD-ROM   A compact optical disc, similar in appearance to an audio CD, that can store over 500 MB of information that can be viewed but cannot be changed. A CD-ROM drive is needed to read the data on a CD-ROM disc.

client-server network   A arrangement of workstations that are connected to a central computer, or server. The server does the bulk of the work in sharing resources and transferring information across the network cabling.

cluster   A group of sectors on a computer hard disk. A cluster is the smallest unit used for storing a file or part of a file. While a cluster is fixed in size for a given disk, a file can be any size, up to the limits of the operating system. When you save a file, it is stored in the first available cluster. When that cluster is filled, the remainder of the file is stored in the next available clusters on the disk.

communication port   Typically, an external connector at the back of a computer system that can be used to connect a modem. *See also* port.

component   A feature or accessory of Windows 95, such as the System Resource Monitor or Notepad, that you can install or remove from your system. The components selected for each installation type are not the only components that you can install. Some components are installed by every installation type, but no installation option installs every component.

compressed volume file A file created by DriveSpace that appears as a new hard drive, with approximately twice the capacity as the original drive.

Control Panel The set of Windows 95 programs you can use to change system, hardware, software, and Windows 95 settings.

conversation On The Microsoft Network, a conversation is one topic on a bulletin board that includes a main message as well as all of its responses.

defragment To place all of the related pieces, or fragments, of a disk file into one contiguous stream.

Desktop The entire Windows 95 screen that represents your work area in Windows 95. Icons, windows, and the taskbar are displayed on the Windows 95 Desktop. You can customize the Desktop to suit your preferences and working requirements.

destination A document or program into which an object is embedded or linked.

dial-up client A computer that initiates a phone call to a remote computer through a phone line.

Dial-Up Networking The Windows 95 accessory you use to connect two computers that each have a modem.

digital video A file that contains a recording of a moving picture. It is similar in effect to a videotape recording of an event. Some digital video files can also contain an audio recording, so that you can play back both sound and picture.

disk compression A process of reducing the space occupied by the data on your disk. Often you can double the total disk capacity of your hard disk by using a disk compression program, such as DriveSpace.

download To transfer a file from a remote computer to your local computer. This type of transfer can be done with computers on a network or through telecommunication.

electronic mail Notes, messages, and files sent between different computers that use telecommunication or network services. Also referred to as e-mail.

embed To insert an object, which is not linked to its originating (or source) document into a destination document. To edit the embedded object, you double-click it to open the source program within the destination document.

Explorer *See* Windows Explorer.

file server *See* server.

folder A container in which document and program files are stored on your disks. In MS-DOS, a folder was referred to as a directory.

forum   In The Microsoft Network, a forum is a collection of related information on various topics, such as sports, finance, or culture. The information in a forum can appear in several formats, such as a conversation on a bulletin board or in a chat room.

full access   An attribute of a disk volume, folder, or file stored on a shared, network computer that is made available to other users on the network. Full access allows users to make any changes to the volume, folder, or file. *See also* read-only.

graphical user interface   A pictorial representation on a computer screen of the files, data, devices, and programs stored on the computer. A user can issue commands to the computer by interacting with the graphic images displayed on the screen.

host drive   The physical hard drive that contains a compressed volume file.

HyperText Markup Language (HTML)   A standard used to create text files with special codes that any Web browser can retrieve and display.

icon   A small graphic that represents a Windows 95 element, such as a program, a disk drive, or a document. When you double-click an icon, the item the icon represents opens.

Internet   A communication system that connects many different online services and other computer networks throughout the world.

jaggies   The stairstep effect that can appear on graphic images that are enlarged.

jump   An underlined word or phrase on a Web page that, when clicked, takes you to another location on the World Wide Web.

Local Area Network (LAN)   A network composed of the workstations in your local office or group. *See also* Wide Area Network.

lost cluster   A partial file fragment which is not associated with any file on the disk. A lost cluster takes up file space, but it does not show up in any file listings.

map   To designate a shared folder or drive on a network computer as a drive available to your computer. When you map a folder or drive, you create a new drive on your computer through which you can use shared resources on the network computer.

Microsoft Exchange   The Windows 95 program you can use to send and receive electronic mail, faxes, and files on a network or online service. Microsoft Exchange acts as a central "post office" for all messaging activities.

Microsoft Network, The   *See* The Microsoft Network.

modem   A hardware device that converts digital computer information into audio signals that can be sent through phone lines. These signals are received and converted back to digital signals by the receiving modem.

MS-DOS–based program   A program designed to run under MS-DOS.

Musical Instrument Digital Interface (MIDI) A format for sound files for playback on MIDI devices. A MIDI file is not a recording of a sound; it is a set of instructions about what instruments play the sound, and then what notes to play.

My Computer The Windows 95 program that you can use to browse through your computer's filing system, and to open drives, folders, and files. You can also use My Computer to manage your files and your filing system, by moving, copying, renaming, and deleting items.

network client A software program that provides the connection between your workstation and the network.

network drive A shared folder or drive on the network that you have mapped to your computer. A network drive is represented by a network drive icon. You can use this icon to open and use the files and folders stored in that drive. *See also* map.

Network Neighborhood The Windows 95 program you can use to explore the network to which your computer is connected.

network A system of multiple computers that uses special networking programs to share files, software, printers, and other resources among the different computers that are connected in the network.

newsgroup A collection of messages and responses on related topics on the Internet. It is similar to bulletin boards on The Microsoft Network.

online service A subscription computer service that you can use to access information and talk with other users. You can obtain reports on news, sports, weather, the stock market, and more. You can also do research, and send mail to other users of the service.

password A unique series of characters that you type to gain entry into a restricted network system, an electronic mail system, or a protected folder or file. Passwords are used to protect the security of the information stored on a computer.

path The location of a file within a computer filing system. The path indicates the disk drive, folder, subfolders, and filename in which the file is stored. If the path indicates a file on another computer on a network, it also includes the computer name.

PC card A Personal Computer Memory Card International Association (PCMCIA) device, such as a modem or network connection, contained on a card approximately the size of a credit card. PC cards enable computers, especially portable computers, to have additional accessories installed without restarting Windows 95.

peer-to-peer network A network in which all the workstations have equal access to each other, all can share resources, and all share the workload of transferring information across the network cabling.

Plug and Play A feature of Windows 95 and newer computer systems that enables your computer to detect the devices installed on your computer. It is designed to make the process of installing new hardware on computers easier.

point-to-point protocol (PPP) A communication method used by a variety of servers and systems for remote connections.

port A socket or slot that is a connector to your computer system unit into which you can plug the adapter for a hardware device, such as a printer, hard disk, modem, or mouse.

private folder A folder stored on a shared, network computer that has not been designated as available to other users on the network. Only the user who created the folder can open, view, or edit the files in a private folder.

program file A file that stores detailed computer instructions that make a program operational.

program A detailed set of computer instructions that you can use to perform related tasks, such as composing a letter with a word processing program, calculating a column of figures with a spreadsheet program, or backing up files with a system utility program.

public folder A folder stored on a shared, network computer that is made available to other users on the network.

read-only An attribute of a disk volume, folder, or file stored on a shared, network computer that is made available to other users on the network. An item designated as read-only allows users to view files, but not edit the files. *See also* full access.

Recycle Bin The Windows 95 program that holds files, folders, and other items you have deleted. Recycle Bin is represented by an icon on the Desktop. Until Recycle Bin is "emptied," you can recover items you have deleted or placed in Recycle Bin.

remote access protocol A software program that controls how data is transmitted from a dial-up client to a remote computer.

ScanDisk The Windows 95 accessory that checks a disk or disk drive for faults or errors.

sector A section on a disk. Each sector stores the same amount of information, typically 512 bytes.

server A central computer on certain types of networks to which all computers on the network are connected, and through which users can obtain shared network resources.

shared resource Hardware, software, or information that users on a network have identified as being available to other users, for example, a public folder, a file server, or a network printer.

shortcut menu A menu that lists commands that directly apply to the action you are performing. Many shortcut menus are accessed by clicking the Desktop or a program element with the right mouse button.

shortcut   An easily accessible icon that represents and points to a program, folder, or file stored elsewhere on the computer. You can place a shortcut anywhere you can place a file or folder such as on your Desktop, Start menu, or Programs menu.

Start button   The command button in the lower-left corner of the Windows 95 Desktop. The Start button serves as the starting point from which all Windows 95 programs, activities, and functions begin.

Start menu   The menu that presents commands that are a starting point for all work you do on your computer, such as starting a program, opening a document, finding a file, getting help, and so forth. You open the Start menu by clicking the Start button displayed on the Desktop.

status bar   The bar at the bottom of a program window that indicates the program status, for example, the page number, current mode, object size, and so forth. The display of the status bar can often be turned on and off.

swap file   The swap file is used by Windows 95 to temporarily copy data that is located in memory to your hard disk, thereby making that memory available for more data or programs. When the data in the swap file is needed by a program Windows 95 will copy the data back into memory. A swap file makes your computer appear to have more memory than is actually installed.

tab dialog box   A type of dialog box divided into two or more categories, which can be accessed by clicking the named tabs at the top of the dialog box.

taskbar   The rectangular bar usually located across the bottom of the Windows 95 Desktop. The taskbar includes the Start button as well as buttons for any programs and documents that are open. Its location, size, and visibility can be modified to fit your preferences.

The Microsoft Network   The online service included with Windows 95. *See also* online service.

Uniform Resource Location (URL)   The address of a page on the World Wide Web.

upload   To transfer a file from a user's local computer to a network computer, or to another centrally located computer, perhaps accessed through telecommunication.

user profile   A collection of settings that are specific to each user. For example, you might have one setting for yourself, and another for your assistant. By enabling user profiles, each user who logs on to Windows 95 at your workstation can keep his or her settings separate.

Web browser   A program that formats and displays files on the World Wide Web. These files can display text, pictures, sound, or jumps to other locations on the World Wide Web. *See also* HyperText Markup Language.

Wide Area Network (WAN)   A set of workstations in your local office or group as well as the workstation located in remote offices or other sites. *See also* Local Area Network.

Windows Explorer   The Windows 95 program you can use to browse through, open, and manage the disk drives, folders, and files on your computer. In a network system, you can also use Windows Explorer to view and open shared folders on other computers on the network. You can use Windows Explorer to manage your files by moving, copying, renaming, and deleting files.

Windows-based program   A program designed to run on the Windows operating system. *See also* MS-DOS–based program.

workstation   A computer connected to a network.

World Wide Web (WWW)   A set of locations, accessed through addresses, on the Internet that can be viewed using various products, such as a Web browser. *See also* Web browser.

Index

IMPORTANT — READ CAREFULLY BEFORE OPENING SOFTWARE PACKET(S).
By opening the sealed packet(s) containing the software, you indicate your acceptance
of the following Microsoft License Agreement.

Microsoft License Agreement

MICROSOFT LICENSE AGREEMENT
(Single User Products)

This is a legal agreement between you (either an individual or an entity) and Microsoft Corporation. By opening the sealed software packet(s) you are agreeing to be bound by the terms of this agreement. If you do not agree to the terms of this agreement, promptly return the book, including the unopened software packet(s), to the place you obtained it for a full refund.

MICROSOFT SOFTWARE LICENSE

1. GRANT OF LICENSE. Microsoft grants to you the right to use one copy of the Microsoft software program included with this book (the "SOFTWARE") on a single terminal connected to a single computer. The SOFTWARE is in "use" on a computer when it is loaded into temporary memory (i.e., RAM) or installed into permanent memory (e.g., hard disk, CD-ROM, or other storage device) of that computer. You may not network the SOFTWARE or otherwise use it on more than one computer or computer terminal at the same time.

2. COPYRIGHT. The SOFTWARE is owned by Microsoft or its suppliers and is protected by United States copyright laws and international treaty provisions. Therefore, you must treat the SOFTWARE like any other copyrighted material (e.g., a book or musical recording) except that you may either (a) make one copy of the SOFTWARE solely for backup or archival purposes, or (b) transfer the SOFTWARE to a single hard disk provided you keep the original solely for backup or archival purposes. You may not copy the written materials accompanying the SOFTWARE.

3. OTHER RESTRICTIONS. You may not rent or lease the SOFTWARE, but you may transfer the SOFTWARE and accompanying written materials on a permanent basis provided you retain no copies and the recipient agrees to the terms of this Agreement. You may not reverse engineer, decompile, or disassemble the SOFTWARE. If the SOFTWARE is an update or has been updated, any transfer must include the most recent update and all prior versions.

4. DUAL MEDIA SOFTWARE. If the SOFTWARE package contains both 3.5" and 5.25" disks, then you may use only the disks appropriate for your single-user computer. You may not use the other disks on another computer or loan, rent, lease, or transfer them to another user except as part of the permanent transfer (as provided above) of all SOFTWARE and written materials.

5. LANGUAGE SOFTWARE. If the SOFTWARE is a Microsoft language product, then you have a royalty-free right to reproduce and distribute executable files created using the SOFTWARE. If the language product is a Basic or COBOL product, then Microsoft grants you a royalty-free right to reproduce and distribute the run-time modules of the SOFTWARE provided that you: (a) distribute the run-time modules only in conjunction with and as a part of your software product; (b) do not use Microsoft's name, logo, or trademarks to market your software product; (c) include a valid copyright notice on your software product; and (d) agree to indemnify, hold harmless, and defend Microsoft and its suppliers from and against any claims or lawsuits, including attorneys' fees, that arise or result from the use or distribution of your software product. The "run-time modules" are those files in the SOFTWARE that are identified in the accompanying written materials as required during execution of your software program. The run-time modules are limited to run-time files, install files, and ISAM and REBUILD files. If required in the SOFTWARE documentation, you agree to display the designated patent notices on the packaging and in the README file of your software product.

LIMITED WARRANTY

LIMITED WARRANTY. Microsoft warrants that (a) the SOFTWARE will perform substantially in accordance with the accompanying written materials for a period of ninety (90) days from the date of receipt, and (b) any hardware accompanying the SOFTWARE will be free from defects in materials and workmanship under normal use and service for a period of one (1) year from the date of receipt. Any implied warranties on the SOFTWARE and hardware are limited to ninety (90) days and one (1) year, respectively. Some states/countries do not allow limitations on duration of an implied warranty, so the above limitation may not apply to you.

CUSTOMER REMEDIES. Microsoft's and its suppliers' entire liability and your exclusive remedy shall be, at Microsoft's option, either (a) return of the price paid, or (b) repair or replacement of the SOFTWARE or hardware that does not meet Microsoft's Limited Warranty and which is returned to Microsoft with a copy of your receipt. This Limited Warranty is void if failure of the SOFTWARE or hardware has resulted from accident, abuse, or misapplication. Any replacement SOFTWARE or hardware will be warranted for the remainder of the original warranty period or thirty (30) days, whichever is longer. Outside the United States, these remedies are not available without proof of purchase from an authorized non-U.S. source.

NO OTHER WARRANTIES. Microsoft and its suppliers disclaim all other warranties, either express or implied, including, but not limited to implied warranties of merchantability and fitness for a particular purpose, with regard to the SOFTWARE, the accompanying written materials, and any accompanying hardware. This limited warranty gives you specific legal rights. You may have others which vary from state/country to state/country.

NO LIABILITY FOR CONSEQUENTIAL DAMAGES. In no event shall Microsoft or its suppliers be liable for any damages whatsoever (including without limitation, damages for loss of business profits, business interruption, loss of business information, or any other pecuniary loss) arising out of the use of or inability to use this Microsoft product, even if Microsoft has been advised of the possibility of such damages. Because some states/countries do not allow the exclusion or limitation of liability for consequential or incidental damages, the above limitation may not apply to you.

U.S. GOVERNMENT RESTRICTED RIGHTS

The SOFTWARE and documentation are provided with RESTRICTED RIGHTS. Use, duplication, or disclosure by the Government is subject to restrictions as set forth in subparagraph (c)(1)(ii) of The Rights in Technical Data and Computer Software clause at DFARS 252.227-7013 or subparagraphs (c)(1) and (2) of the Commercial Computer Software — Restricted Rights 48 CFR 52.227-19, as applicable. Manufacturer is Microsoft Corporation, One Microsoft Way, Redmond, WA 98052-6399. This Agreement is governed by the laws of the State of Washington.

Should you have any questions concerning this Agreement, or if you desire to contact Microsoft for any reason, please write: Microsoft Sales and Service, One Microsoft Way, Redmond, WA 98052-6399.

CORPORATE ORDERS

If you're placing a large-volume corporate
order for additional copies of this
Step by Step title, or for any other
Microsoft Press book, you may be eligible
for our corporate discount.

Call **1-800-888-3303, ext. 62669,** for details.

097-000-681

The

Step by Step

Practice Files Disk

The enclosed 3.5-inch disk contains timesaving, ready-to-use practice files that complement the lessons in this book. To use the practice files, you'll need the Windows 95 operating system.

Each *Step by Step* lesson uses practice files from the disk. Before you begin the *Step by Step* lessons, read the "Getting Ready" section of the book for easy instructions telling how to install the files on your computer's hard disk. As you work through each lesson, be sure to follow the instructions for renaming the practice files so that you can go through a lesson more than once if you need to.

Please take a few moments to read the License Agreement on the previous page before using the enclosed disk.

Register your Microsoft Press® book today, and let us know what you think.

At Microsoft Press, we listen to our customers. We update our books as new releases of software are issued, and we'd like you to tell us the kinds of additional information you'd find most useful in these updates. Your feedback will be considered when we prepare a future edition; plus, when you become a registered owner, you'll get Microsoft Press catalogs and exclusive offers on specially priced books.

Thanks!

I used this book as
- ⬤ A way to learn the software
- ⬤ A reference when I needed it
- ⬤ A way to find out about advanced features
- ⬤ Other_____

I consider myself
- ⬤ A beginner or an occasional computer user
- ⬤ An intermediate-level user with a pretty good grasp of the basics
- ⬤ An advanced user who helps and provides solutions for others
- ⬤ Other_____

I purchased this book from
- ⬤ A bookstore
- ⬤ A software store
- ⬤ A direct mail offer
- ⬤ Other_____

I will buy the next edition of the book when it's updated
- ⬤ Definitely
- ⬤ Probably
- ⬤ I will not buy the next edition

The next edition of this book should include the following additional information:

1| _____
2| _____
3| _____

The most useful things about this book are _____

_____

This book would be more helpful if_____

_____

My general impressions of this book are _____

_____

May we contact you regarding your comments? ⬤ Yes   ⬤ No
Would you like to receive a Microsoft Press catalog regularly? ⬤ Yes   ⬤ No

Name _____

Company (if applicable) _____

Address _____

City_____ State _____ Zip _____

Daytime phone number (optional)_(_____)_____

Please mail back your feedback form—postage free! Fold this form as
described on the other side of this card, or fax this sheet to:
Microsoft Press, Attn: Marketing Department, fax 206-936-7329

FOLD HERE

NO POSTAGE
NECESSARY
IF MAILED
IN THE
UNITED STATES

BUSINESS REPLY MAIL
FIRST-CLASS MAIL   PERMIT NO. 108   REDMOND, WA

POSTAGE WILL BE PAID BY ADDRESSEE

ATTN: MARKETING DEPT
MICROSOFT PRESS
ONE MICROSOFT WAY
REDMOND WA 98052-9953

FOLD HERE